Dominate Your Local Google Search

A Step-by-Step Guide For Local Businesses
How To Be #1 In Google In Your Local Market

Dominate Your Local Google Search

A Step-by-Step Guide For Local Businesses How To Be #1 In Google In Your Local Market

Ray Riechert, Jerry Riechert,
Scott Morris and Kathy Roberts

Freeze Time Media

ISBN-10:0-9966883-4-X

ISBN-13:978-0-9966883-4-5

Freeze Time Media

Cover illustration by Jaz Escamilla

Contents

Introduction

Everybody's heard of Google, and everybody's used Google, so if you own or manage a small business, why aren't you dominating your Local Google Search?

For most business owners and managers the answer is simply that they don't know how or didn't know they could dominate the top of their Local Google Search.

Well, not only is it possible, but it's essential to your success, and it can make or break your business.

A Google search precedes 87% of all visits to a local business.

Most businesses advertise in one form or another, but potential customers who hear or see your ad often don't remember your name. What they most often remember is your message, so they go to Google and type in "keywords" that they remember from your message, and bingo, there you are; or maybe I should say, "there you should be."

When potential customers type keywords into the Google search field that relate to your business, if your website, video, blog or other online real estate doesn't pop up, you're dust.

The good news is that never has to happen.

In this book, we have detailed every step you need to take to get ranked #1 in Local Google Search every time. We hold nothing back; we reveal all the secrets so that you can do it yourself for your own business.

If you would like more information on our premium services and "Done-for-You" services please visit us at www.localbusinessassociates.com/services

Why are we sharing all our secrets?

Because we know that some people won't want to do it themselves and will potentially use some of our premium "paid for" services, and that's how we make money. But we're giving you all the information right here, right now, with absolutely nothing left out.

So, enjoy the next 80 pages of this awesome book and please let us hear of your success with our information.

Your next stop = #1 in Local Google Search

Thanks,

Ray, Scott, Jerry and Kathy

Getting Free Advertising on Google

Why Buy Local?

Over the past few years, customers have decided to support their local businesses over the big box stores more and more. The reasons are obvious. Local businesses provide a better experience.

Data collected from AYTM Market Research in 2014 demonstrated that personal service was the second most important reason Internet users chose local businesses over larger corporate companies by 53%.

Lower prices offered by big box stores didn't always mean customers would choose that option. In fact, 61% of respondents said they would prefer to support local businesses at the expense of price.

Herein lies the dilemma for local businesses. Online searches have exploded over the past five years, and customers are doing more research prior to making purchases regardless of the business.

The big corporate businesses have a distinct advantage over local businesses because they have much larger budgets to get the word out to customers.

So what do the big box stores do well that your local business needs to be doing?

What Did Studies Show?

In studies done with local businesses in the United States and the United Kingdom, the number one concern business owners had was search engine optimization (SEO).

Think about the number of calls your local business receives from companies telling you they can get you ranked on page one of Google and the other search engines.

There very well could be good companies that can do this for you, but it's equally important to understand how this process works so you can direct them or even do it yourself.

This is where *Local Business Associates* comes in. Our goal is to help you understand how you can leverage the search engines like Google so you can get better rankings so customers can find you online.

Local Business Associates will examine the concepts and ideas that will help you get free advertising from the big search engines like Google and the local search engines like Yelp.

Local Business Associates will also examine other concepts and ideas such as on-page SEO, Name-Address-Phone Number (N.A.P.), citation consistency across the Internet and content creation.

Let's get started and help you get the Internet presence you need to compete against other local businesses.

Search Engine Optimization (SEO)

Every business needs to have an online presence, plain and simple. If you believe you can do just fine without a presence, you're risking the chance that one of your competitors is doing more than you to get found online.

Here's an example of a barbecue restaurant in Austin, Texas:

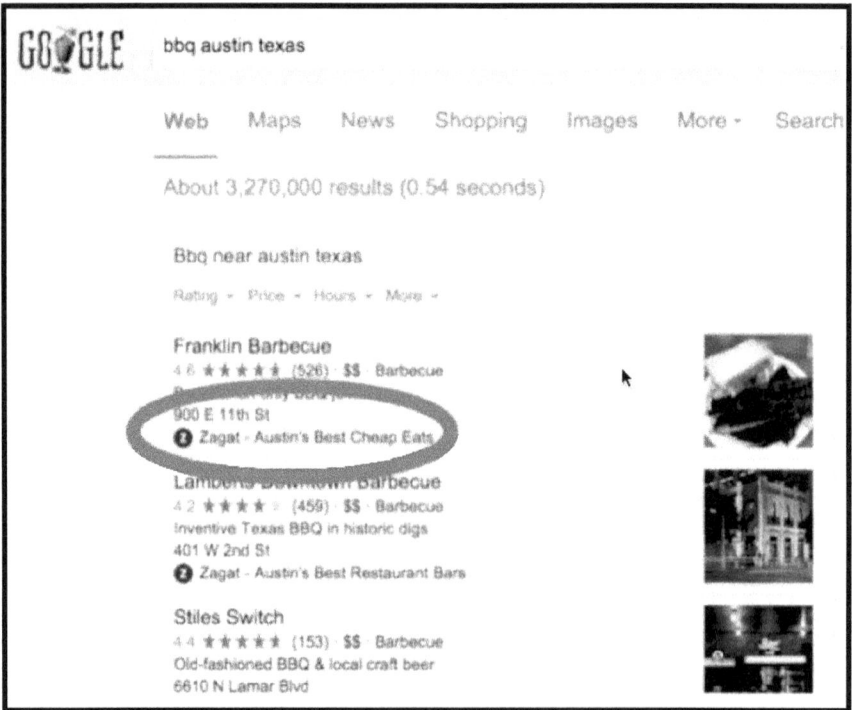

GOOGLE
brisket austin texas
Web
Shopping
Images
News
Maps
More
Search
About 202,000 results (0.56 seconds)
Brisket near austin texas
Rating · Price · Hours · More
Franklin Barbecue
4.6 ★★★★★ (526) · $$ · Barbecue
Zagat - Austin's Best Cheap Eats
La Barbecue
3 reviews · Restaurant
1906 E Cesar Chavez St
Fullhouse bbq
No reviews · Barbecue

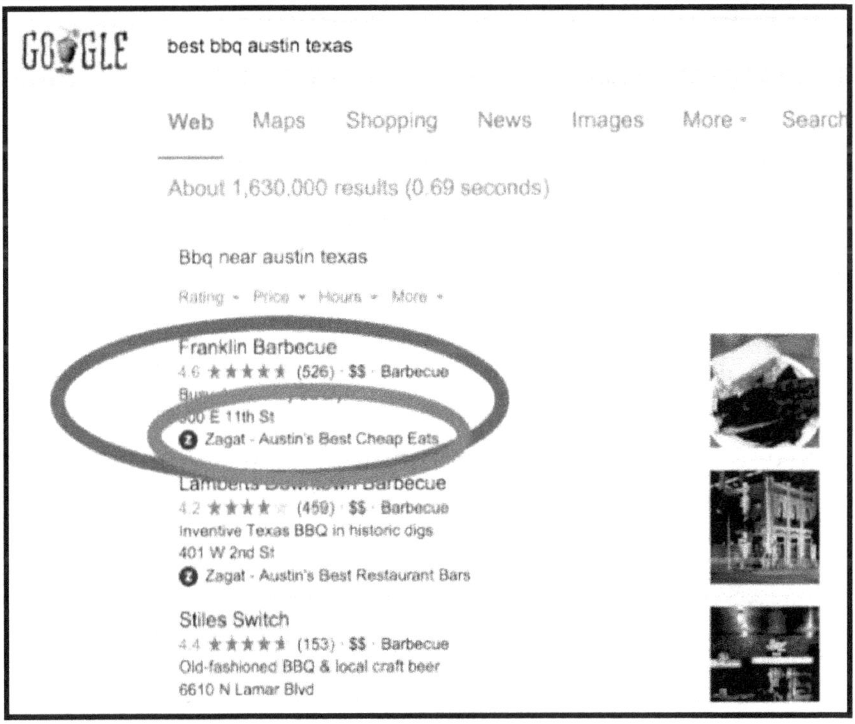
GOOGLE
best bbq austin texas
Web
Maps
Shopping
News
Images
More
About 1,630,000 results (0.69 seconds)
Bbq near austin texas
Rating · Price · Hours · More
Franklin Barbecue
4.6 ★★★★★ (526) · $$ · Barbecue
Zagat - Austin's Best Cheap Eats
4.2 ★★★★ (459) · $$ · Barbecue
Inventive Texas BBQ in historic digs
401 W 2nd St
Zagat - Austin's Best Restaurant Bars
Stiles Switch
4.4 ★★★★★ (153) · $$ · Barbecue
Old-fashioned BBQ & local craft beer
6610 N Lamar Blvd

3 Things You Should Know About the Google 3-Pack

Here are three things you should recognize on these three Google searches. First, Google has recently changed from a 7-pack of businesses to a 3-pack of businesses. Unfortunately, this makes getting FREE prime space on Google a little tougher.

Second, the search terms we used here are typical of the types of searches anyone would enter in Google. Keywords aren't used in these three examples.

And third, you'll notice that Franklin Barbecue is the first listing on all three searches.

Why does Franklin Barbecue show up in the very first listing for barbecue restaurants in Austin, Texas?

Franklin Barbecue may have some advantages other barbecue restaurants in Austin don't have. For example, they're featured on national TV ads, they've been featured on national TV shows and they may have great word of mouth that is evidenced by the long lines that form outside their business everyday.

The most important thing you have to realize is that every person on the planet who searches the Internet searches differently. This means you have opportunities to get found with other search terms or be in the second or third spot.

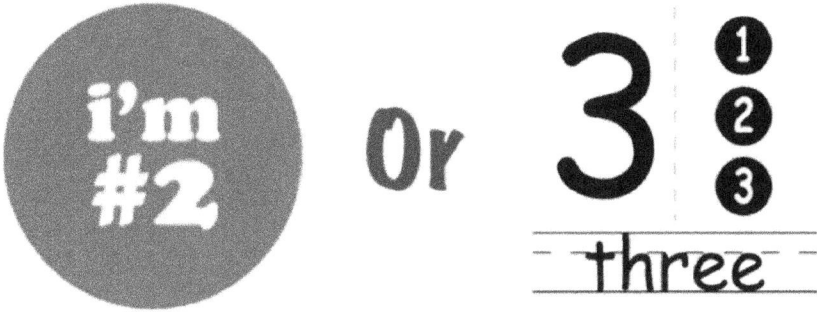

Why Should You Get in the Google 3-Pack

Your goal is to get into one of the three top spots. This will help your business tremendously because you're getting FREE advertising.

Depending on the business type you're in and where you're located will determine the amount of work required to achieve a top three position.

You may be wondering why this is important.

Think about the amount of money you spend on advertising through TV, radio, coupons, newspapers, postcards, etc. There's no doubt you're paying a lot of money with varying results.

Achieving a top three position on Google is very important because it's FREE, and most people will do some research before they buy goods and services from you.

Two Types of Keywords You Should Use

Local Business Associates recommends two types of keywords because that's what Google and YouTube recommend.

The first are keywords found in Google's Keyword Planner. This service is FREE as long as you sign up for a Google AdWords account.

Google and YouTube account for about 68% of all search, and these numbers are as accurate as you'll get. For local businesses, keywords are fairly simple.

Let's take a look at the Google Keyword Planner to show you that this isn't as mysterious as you may think.

You'll start by searching for the Keyword Planner on Google. Then you have several options. You'll want to choose "Search for new keywords using a phrase, website or category."

It's best to use a broad term to get started because the Keyword Planner will do the work for you. So keep your broad term to 1-3 words only.

Google   google keyword planner

Web   Apps   Videos   News   Images   More ·   Search

About 964,000 results (0.24 seconds)

Keyword research tool: - SEMrush.com
[Ad] www.semrush.com/Keyword_Tool ▾
Over 80,000,000 keywords in SEMrush US database! Start your
free trial
29 databases · 670,000 users · 80 million keywords in US · 46...

Google Keyword Planner - Google.com
[Ad] www.google.com/AdWords ▾
Find Keywords to Target Your Ads. Visit the AdWords ™ Official
Site.
Free Lifetime Support · No Budget Minimums · Advertise On Y...
Services: Google AdWords, AdWords Express, Google Displa...
What Does It Cost? - How AdWords Works - Why Choose Ad...

Google AdWords: Keyword Planner
https://adwords.google.com/KeywordPlanner ▾ Google ·
Keyword Planner is a free AdWords tool that helps you build
Search Network campaigns by finding keyword ideas and
estimating how they may perform.
You've visited this page many times. Last visit: 10/31/15

Using Keyword Planner to g...   Sign in
Keyword Planner is like a   Sign in to continue to
workshop for building new   Google AdWords. Email
...   Password Stay ...

More results from google.com »

Keyword Planner

Where would you like to start?

Find new keywords and get search volume data

> ‣ Search for new keywords using a phrase, website or category

> ‣ Get search volume data and trends

> ‣ Multiply keyword lists to get new keywords

Plan your budget and get forecasts

> ‣ Get click and cost performance forecasts

Keyword Planner
Where would you like to start?

🔍 Find new keywords and get search volume data

- Search for new keywords using a phrase, website or category

Enter one or more of the following:
Your product or service

plumber

Your landing page

www.example.com/page

Your product category

Enter or select a product category

Targeting	Customize your search
Denver	**Keyword filters**
English	**Keyword options**
Google	Show broadly related ideas
Negative keywords	Hide keywords in my account
	Hide keywords in my plan
Date range	**Keywords to include**
Show avg. monthly searches for: Last 12 months	

Get Ideas ⬅

Always Start Your Search with a Broad Term

In this example, we use the broad term "plumber." And since we're talking about local businesses, it's important to use a city or town name in the "Targeting" section.

In this example, we chose Denver because it will typically pick up the surrounding cities and towns too. Recently, Google has changed its algorithm to narrow the radius for any given business.

The radius is something Google doesn't publish, but for brick and mortar stores the radius depends on the density of the population.

For example, in major cities like New York, Chicago, Houston or Los Angeles, the radius will be small, whereas in more rural settings the radius will be larger.

If you run a service area business like plumbing, painting and construction, you're allowed to add ZIP codes of your surrounding cities and towns on Google Plus for Business (Google My Business).

This is a very good feature that Google finally put in place. But you have to keep in mind that customers will likely stick with service area businesses in their town first because they don't think you will come to their town.

Okay, now that we've discussed some basic information about the Google Keyword Planner, let's look at the results for the term "plumber."

You should look at a few things on the search result. First, "plumber" is the word we searched at the top left-hand corner of the screen. Make sure you click on "Keyword Ideas" because when you start the search it automatically defaults to "Ad Group Ideas."

You'll notice that we've highlighted a box in the top right-hand corner. You can click on this to download up to 801 keywords at a time. This is the reason you want to sign up for a Google AdWords account.

As we work our way down the page, you'll see an "arrow" pointing to "Avg. Monthly Searches." If you click on this term once it will switch your searches from high to low, and if you click on it twice it will go from low to high.

We've highlighted a few of the keyword terms. The ones with the word "Denver" in them are particularly valuable because people are actually typing these into a search on Google.

Don't worry when you see a search term like "plumbers Denver" because Google doesn't care about filler words like it, a, an and the.

Here's a good example that you can use in your content using "plumbers Denver":

"Diamond Jim's Plumbing is one of the leading and most respected *plumbers* in *Denver*."

Google will spider your content and find the term "plumbers Denver" because people are searching for it at least 480 times per month. This is also a great keyword because plumbing businesses are willing to pay $85 every time someone clicks on that ad.

FREE Traffic is Key to Your Internet Presence

The goal of *Local Business Associates* is always to get you as much FREE traffic as possible without paying Google to use their AdWords ads.

Think of it this way: Would you rather pay $85 every time someone clicks on your ad (you are charged $85 even if they don't take an action) or would you like to get FREE traffic because you can be found in one of the top three spots on Google?

Will Semantic Text Help You or Hurt You?

There's another type of keyword that Google expects you to use. Semantic text are keywords that have the same meaning as keywords you find on the Google Keyword Planner except these are words you will need to develop.

Since we're talking about plumbers in Denver, let's come up with semantic text.

"Diamond Jim's *Plumbing of Denver* fixes leaky faucets, replaces old water heaters and cleans your drains in the event that you need emergency plumbing."

The key to using semantic text is to brand your business and connect it with a city, town or neighborhood. In this example, plumbing and Denver mean the same thing as the Google Keyword Planner keyword "plumbers Denver."

Be Creative, Don't Always Stay in the Box

Google knows people searching the Internet for plumbers aren't going to always use the keywords found in the Keyword Planner.

This means it's up to you to be creative in writing content that has a mixture of both types of keywords so when the search engine spiders visit your site, they know exactly what you're talking about.

There's a term called "keyword stuffing." Many service area businesses use this hoping that it will help them with search engines like Google.

Here are two examples of keyword stuffing. It may seem important to these plumbing companies to list all their services on the homepage, but that's not necessary.

Forget the "Keyword Stuffing"

Google is looking for great content and plenty of it. Instead of listing every service on the homepage, use the tabs at the top of the homepage and separate the various services into subcategories.

Installation or Repair of Faucet Fixtures

- Kitchen & Bathroom Fixtures Installation & Replacement
- Garbage Disposal Installation or Replacement
- Toilet Replacement, Repair or Installation
- Water Heater Replacement or Installation
- Plumbing Repairs – Complete Service
- Kitchen Remodeling
- Bathroom Remodeling
- Warranty Work
- Maintenance

Products & Services

- Installation or Repair of Faucet Fixtures
- Kitchen & Bathroom Sink Installation & Replacement
- Sump Pump Installation or Replacement
- Garbage Disposal Installation or Replacement
- Toilet Replacement, Repair or Installation
- Water Heater Replacement or Installation
- Sewer Line Repair or Replacement
- Plumbing Repairs – Complete Service
- Kitchen Remodeling
- Bathroom Remodeling
- Warranty Work
- Maintenance

Featured SERVICES

- Sinks/Faucets
- Drains
- Bath Tubs/Showers
- Toilets
- Sewer Lines/Septic Tanks
- Water Pipes
- Water Softeners
- Reverse Osmosis Systems
- Water Heaters
- Garbage Disposals
- Hydro Cleaning Services
- Preventative Maintenance
- Hot Water Recirculation Systems
- Back Flow Prevention
- Grease Traps
- Floor Drains
- Video Inspection
- Gas Lines
- Sewage Ejection Pumps
- Tenant Improvements
- Polybutylene/Galvanized Pipe Replacement

If you would like more information on our premium services and "Done-for-You" services please visit us at www.localbusinessassociates.com/services

How to Beat the Big Boys

The big box stores and large corporations have an advantage over you simply because they have the resources to attract customers.

The good news is that the Internet levels the playing field so that local businesses can compete effectively with the big boys. And Google is there to help you.

Let's look at an example of how a big box store attracts customers:

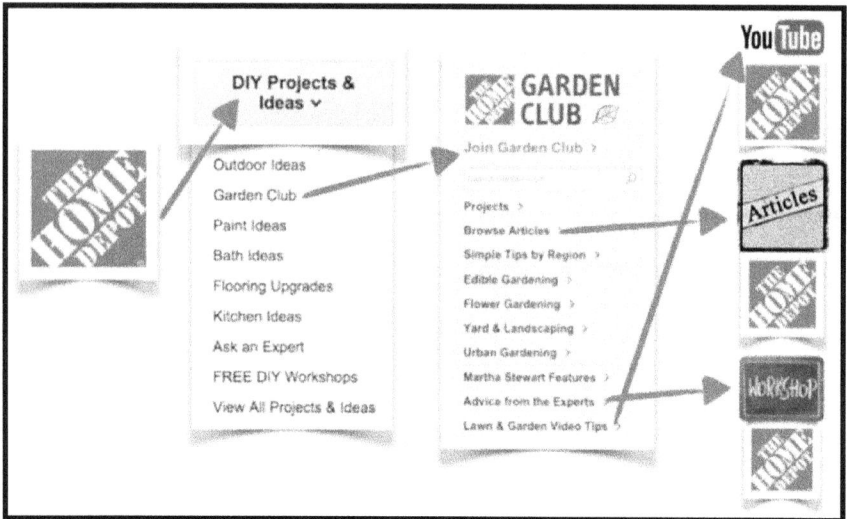

This is a typical pattern that a company like Home Depot uses. They know you will research the products and services you intend to buy.

People are looking for answers and Home Depot uses a structured format to help its customers. For example, a person might be anxious to start landscaping his yard in the spring.

In this example, he will go to the "DIY" tab and choose "Garden Club." The "Garden Club" category offers 10 subcategories. Now the customer feels like he's hit the jackpot.

There's more information than he'll ever need and he'll feel satisfied to a point. Most customers are unsure of how to handle projects, and all the resources in the world won't make any difference unless a qualified person can answer their questions.

Here's a screenshot of Home Depot's homepage:

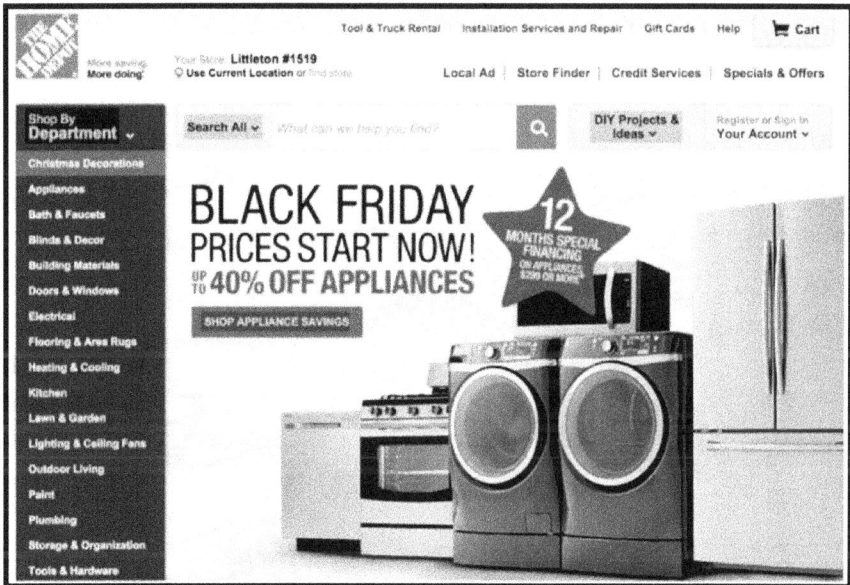

Home Depot focuses on several words:

- Shop
- Search
- DIY

The company knows it has pages and pages of content that will answer most of the questions people have, but can Home Depot get through to the procrastinators and people who are unsure of themselves?

Use the Game Plan of the Big Boys

As a local business owner, you can create a pattern similar to the big boys. The big difference you have going for you is an intimate knowledge of the goods and services you offer.

People are willing to support their local businesses because they're a part of the community and they're friends and neighbors too.

So how do you get started?

First think about the questions you routinely get from your customers. There's a great likelihood that other customers have the same questions.

You have different media to help your customers such as social media, YouTube videos, articles/blogs, images and photos.

If you would like more information on our premium services and "Done-for-You" services please visit us at www.localbusinessassociates.com/services

All the content you add to your website is a way of demonstrating authority. Google loves this and will reward you with higher rankings on local search.

What Would Your Competition Do?

Before you say you don't have time, it's important to realize that customers and potential customers are judging you, and if they don't like what they see, they'll go elsewhere.

Let's take a look at social media first. People are addicted to their cell phones and tablets. In fact, since 2014 searches on smartphones and tablets far outpace searches done on laptops and desktop computers.

Trying to figure out the best way to use social media depends on your type of business. For example, if you own a restaurant it would be very important to use Facebook and Twitter to let your customers know the deals you have going by using photos to show them dishes you serve and encouraging customers to share their experiences with friends.

Social media can also be very unforgiving too. But that isn't a good reason to stay away from it, since many of your competitors are using it to their advantage.

Local businesses that pay attention to their reputation will embrace social media whether comments are positive or negative. Is it frustrating sometimes? You bet it is!

Why Are People So Mean?

You're in business, right? When you expose yourself to social media it's likely that you will have some detractors. It may be your fault or it may be that the customer just wants to hurt you. Who knows?

Regardless of the circumstances, your number one priority is to make the customer feel like he or she is right. You won't do yourself any favors by arguing with a customer.

Every local citation site like Yelp, Merchant Circle, City Search, Trip Advisor, Home Advisor, Red Beacon, Better Business Bureau, etc. allows people to comment on your services and products.

More importantly, they can vent their frustrations out on you. It's a terrible feeling to have someone accuse you of things that aren't true.

If you would like more information on our premium services and "Done-for-You" services please visit us at www.localbusinessassociates.com/services

Your job is to be calm and acknowledge that person's frustrations because it's very unlikely that you'll be able to remove those comments from the citation sites.

Local Business Associates works with a customer that does an excellent job diffusing the situation and understanding that person's point of view.

In this example, Christine responds to several instances on YouTube. It doesn't matter if the comments are on social media sites like YouTube, Facebook, Twitter and Google Plus or the citation sites we mentioned earlier.

Here is the title of the YouTube video:

Clearly, there is a lot of interest in this video since almost 40,000 views were generated in six months!

And there's a BUT. Some people just can't help themselves. They need to introduce negativity into the comment section. So there are a couple of things you can do.

You can ignore it, you can acknowledge the comment positively or you can rip the person for being negative. Keep in mind that other people are going to pay attention to your actions.

If you would like more information on our premium services and "Done-for-You" services please visit us at www.localbusinessassociates.com/services

Here are three separate comments submitted and answered by Christine:

> **Ann Kristin Hansen** 1 month ago
> I like your videos, but its actually difficult to consentrate in what you are saying, because you are talking really, really slow. So slow that I actually are going to leave this video before its finished.
>
> Reply · 3
>
> Hide replies ∧
>
>> **Christine Rich Hanson** 1 month ago
>> +Ann Kristin Hansen Thank you for your feedback. Feminine energy needs to be slower sometimes around a man, then they don't feel like they are in the workplace at home with fast paced talk. My attempt was to show some of that energy for other women. Sorry it didn't feel good to you for listening purposes. I understand. Thank you for liking my videos and stopping in! Take care.

In this comment, the concern seemed legitimate and Christine explained herself and most likely satisfied the viewer.

> **Dora Lee** 2 months ago
> Thank you. I like your video and how at ease you express yourself. I'll try taking your advice and see how it goes.
>
> Reply · 1
>
> View all 3 replies ∨
>
>> **Dora Lee** 4 weeks ago
>> Hi Christine, it has been working well for me, the less I hug and pay attention to him the more he hugs me and wants to be close. your video has been very helpful to me. Thank you so much. Stay beautiful!!
>>
>> Reply · 1
>
>> **Christine Rich Hanson** 3 weeks ago
>> +Dora Lee That is so FANTASTIC Dora!! You took the challenge of doing less and experimented and it worked. Thank you very much for coming back to share. This will help other women as well. Congrats to you Dora!
>>
>> Reply ·

In this example, the comment submitted was positive and she also took the time to say it worked for her. The key to this exchange was that Christine took the time to respond. It may not seem like a big thing, but it probably got her a loyal customer.

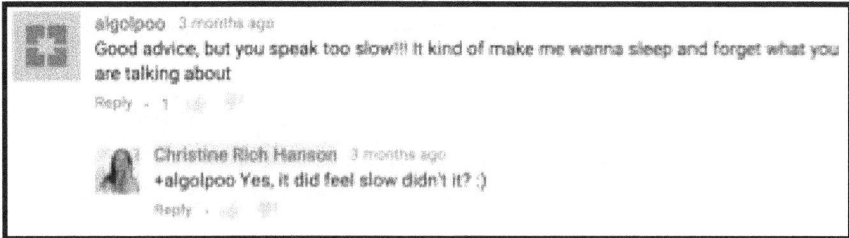

This comment can seem annoying on the surface but is a legitimate comment. Again, Christine does a great job responding. She may not have liked it but she responded and that's what counts.

The Social Media Site You Can't Ignore

Probably the most overlooked social media site is Google Plus for Business and here's why.

Google and YouTube account for 68% of all searches done on the Internet. This means their influence is considerable, and the more you play along with the way Google and YouTube do things, the better off you will be.

You may have a Google Plus account but you probably aren't using it very effectively. That's not a criticism; it's just a reality. But Google rewards those who use their products consistently.

Okay, we know you already have a website and you want to know why Google Plus is important, right?

Right now over 300 million people are currently using Google's social media platform, Google+. Outside the United States, Google+ is the second most used social media platform, seen in over 31 markets, with the United States leading the way, followed by India.

Let's look at an example for emergency plumbing.

When you do a Google search for "emergency plumber Denver," a 3-pack of emergency plumbers will look like this:

Roto-Rooter Plumbing & Drain Services shows up in the number one spot for Denver. However, let's look at what shows up for Highlands Ranch (suburb of Denver).

A very specific scenario will play out when you do a Google search for "emergency plumber Highlands Ranch."

If you would like more information on our premium services and "Done-for-You" services please visit us at www.localbusinessassociates.com/services

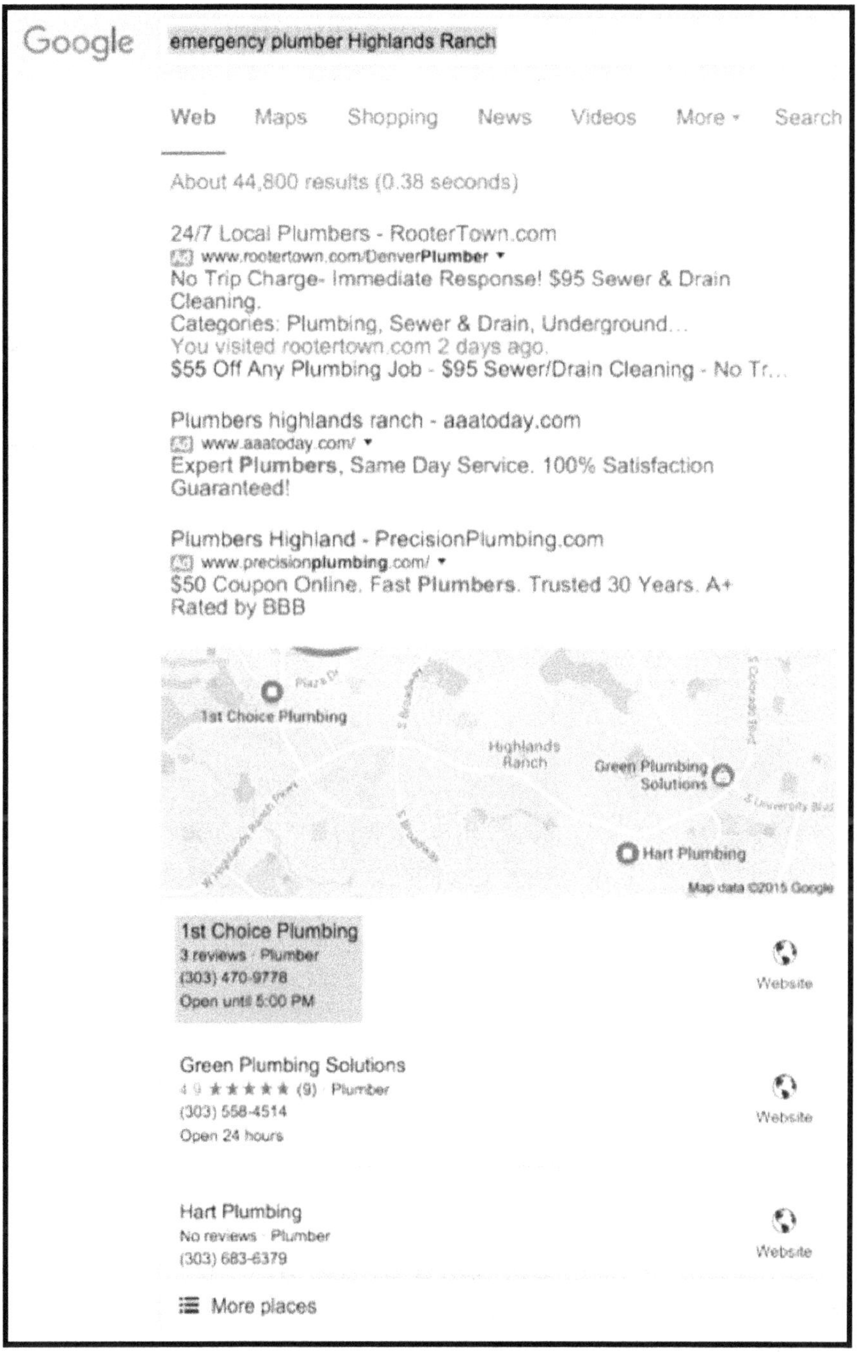
Google
emergency plumber Highlands Ranch
Web
Maps
Shopping
News
Videos
More
Search
About 44,800 results (0.38 seconds)
24/7 Local Plumbers - RooterTown.com
www.rootertown.com/DenverPlumber
No Trip Charge- Immediate Response! $95 Sewer & Drain Cleaning.
Categories: Plumbing, Sewer & Drain, Underground...
You visited rootertown.com 2 days ago.
$55 Off Any Plumbing Job - $95 Sewer/Drain Cleaning - No Tr...
Plumbers highlands ranch - aaatoday.com
www.aaatoday.com/
Expert Plumbers, Same Day Service. 100% Satisfaction Guaranteed!
Plumbers Highland - PrecisionPlumbing.com
www.precisionplumbing.com/
$50 Coupon Online. Fast Plumbers. Trusted 30 Years. A+ Rated by BBB
1st Choice Plumbing
Highlands Ranch
Green Plumbing Solutions
Hart Plumbing
Map data ©2015 Google
1st Choice Plumbing
3 reviews · Plumber
(303) 470-9778
Open until 5:00 PM
Website
Green Plumbing Solutions
4.9 ★★★★★ (9) · Plumber
(303) 558-4514
Open 24 hours
Website
Hart Plumbing
No reviews · Plumber
(303) 683-6379
Website
More places

Now, 1st Choice Plumbing is in the number one position on Google for "emergency plumber."

Google will go with local listings based on the shortest distance to travel and highest reviews. Where do these results come from? Google Plus, of course.

If you want to list your business on Google so you can show up at the top of the SERP (search engine results page), it's essential that you open up a Google+ page for your business.

Google Plus doesn't cost anything. The only thing that's required is verification in the form of a postcard.

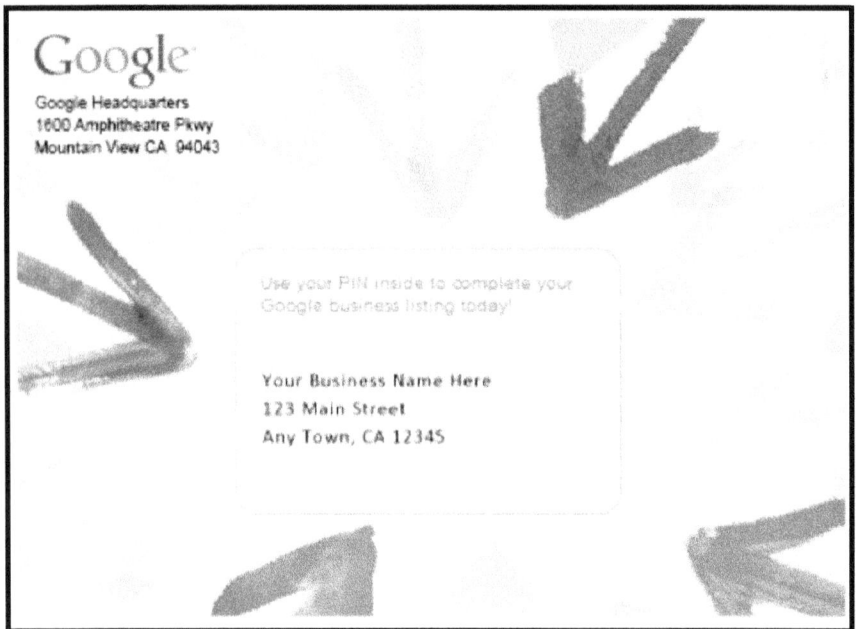

You'll receive this postcard in the mail in one to two weeks. You'll need to enter the PIN on the postcard on your Google Plus page.

If you would like more information on our premium services and "Done-for-You" services please visit us at www.localbusinessassociates.com/services

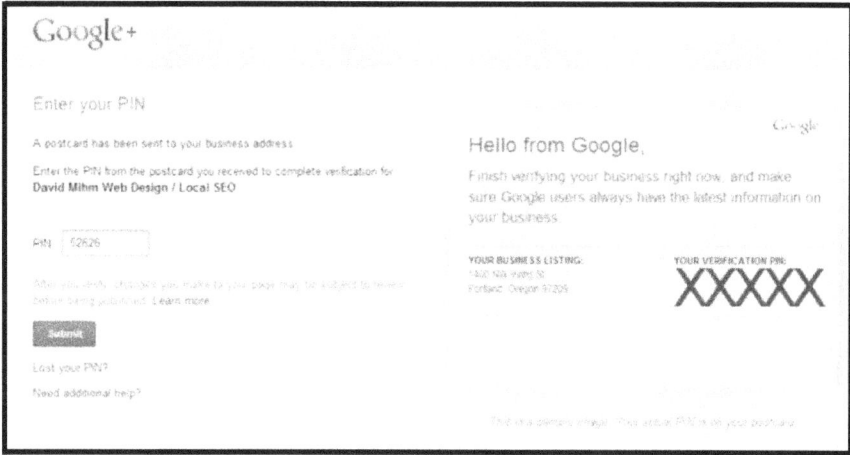

What Will a Google Plus Verification Do?

Once you verify that this is your business, you can begin adding content, videos, images and photos. You can also announce events you can hold live on Google Hangouts and create coupons for sales.

Here are examples of a deep-dish pizza place in Chicago, IL:

The cover for Lou Malnati's Google Plus page is spot on. If you're a fan of deep-dish pizza, who wouldn't get instantly hungry looking at this picture?

Here's an example of one of the posts on Lou Malnati's Google Plus page. Pay attention to the logo in the upper left-hand corner of the page.

Also, look at the +1 at the bottom left-hand corner of the page. Any business that continues to collect +1s from its customers will build authority quickly and get a boost in Google rankings!

Lou Malnati's Pizzeria
Shared publicly · Aug 5, 2015

Deep dish pizza is king around here but a new month brings a new salad! August's Salad of the Month is our Insalata Caprese. Locally grown, vine-ripened tomatoes and fresh mozzarella seasoned with fresh basil and a house-made balsamic vinaigrette. Enjoy August's Salad of the Month while your **#deepdish** is in the oven!

August's
SALAD OF
THE
MONTH

Insalata
caprese

+1

Here are some photos Lou Malnati's posted on its Google Plus page. Photos are important because people love visual things on a page. Plus, all these photos can be tagged for SEO purposes to help boost your business' rankings.

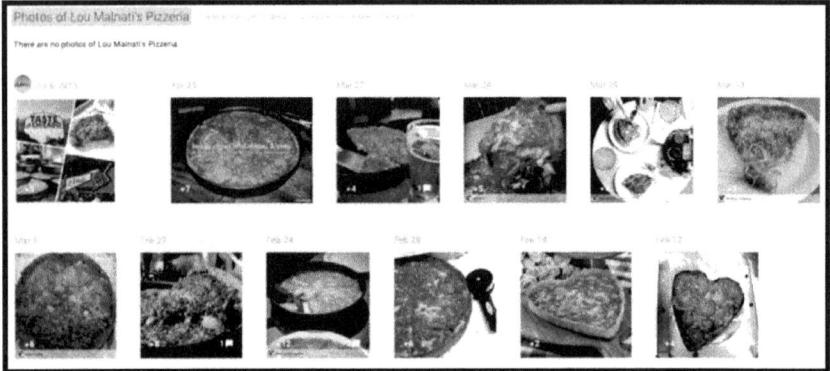

And here are some videos Lou Malnati's posted on YouTube that were automatically added to its Google Plus page.

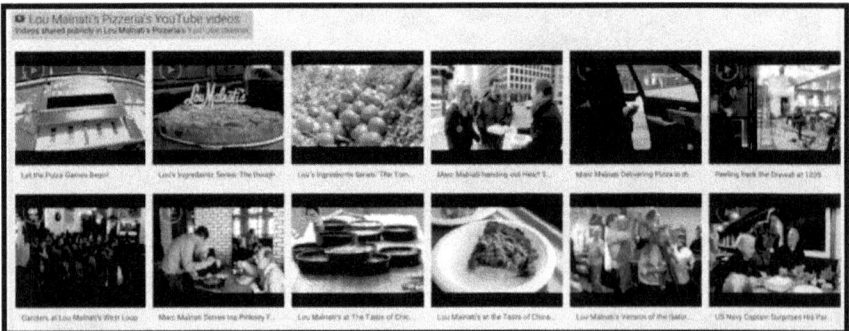

We'll be going into more depth about YouTube videos in another section, but it's worth pointing out that video marketing is the most important marketing strategy being used by large and small businesses across the globe.

You can see that Lou Malnati's Pizzeria has done a tremendous job with its Google Plus page. They've taken complete advantage of the different media strategies available to them.

So if you're looking for a deep-dish pizza place, Lou Malnati's shows up in the number two spot behind another Chicago institution, Giordano's, in an extremely competitive market in Chicago.

This **FREE** advertising will save Lou Malnati's thousands and thousands of dollars in advertising costs each year because they did their work upfront by creating an outstanding Google Plus page.

If you would like more information on our premium services and "Done-for-You" services please visit us at www.localbusinessassociates.com/services

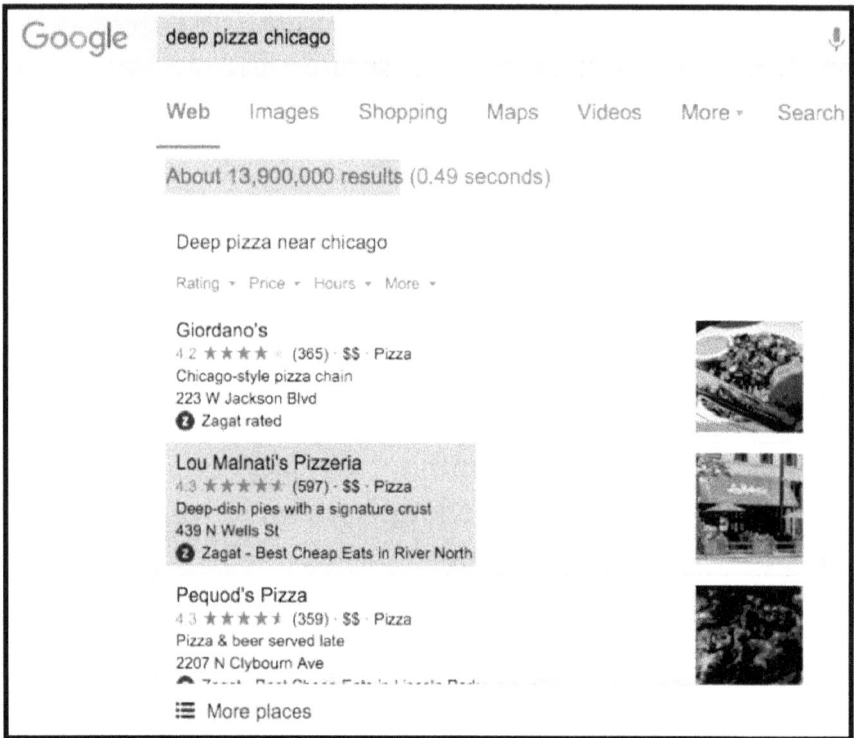

The creation of a **basic** Google Plus page won't net you the results you're looking for though. Google ranks pages higher when the local business puts the time and effort into creating an interactive page.

What Will a Basic Google Plus Page Get You?

We're going to examine a business that didn't put the time or effort into their Google Plus page:

In this example, we'll look at the keyword "Electrician Newark New Jersey." Since we don't live in Newark, we need to add the city and state, otherwise we could be looking at listings in Newark, United Kingdom.

If you would like more information on our premium services and "Done-for-You" services please visit us at www.localbusinessassociates.com/services

electrician newark, NJ

Web   Maps   News   Images   Shopping   More ▾   Search tools

About 307,000 results (0.42 seconds)

newark-electricians.com - Newark NJ Electrician
www.**newark-electricians**.com/ ▾ (201) 812-7373
1 Hour Service - Free Estimates. Lowest Prices In All Of
Newark.
Why Choose Us? · Free Advice & Estimates

Cheap Newark Electricians - homeimprovementexperts.co
www.homeimprovementexperts.co/**Newark** ▾
Electrical Service & Repair Pros. Local & Fast. Quotes are
100% Free!
100% Free Quotes · 24/7 Availability · Same Day Response
Home Addition or Remodel · Wiring or Panel Upgrade · Repair...

Electrician In Newark - Trusted Local Electrician
www.staceyelectric.com/ ▾
30+ Years Experience. Call Us Today!
24 Hour Emergency Service · Membership Discounts
Contact Us · About Us · Testimonials
📍 458 Valley St, City of Orange, NJ - (862) 438-5916

Geronimo Electrical Contractors, Inc.
No reviews · Electrician
(862) 579-3022
Open until 5:00 PM
Website

Proline Electrical Contractors
No reviews · Electrician
26 Paterson St · (973) 522-0444
Website   Directions

Master Electric Services & Maintenance
No reviews · Electrician
40 Mott St · (973) 589-6868
Directions

More places

Newark Electrician
www.thelocalbook.com/**Electrician** ▾
Local, Quality Newark Electricians.
Affordable, Reliable Services Here.

Manhattan Electricians
www.manhattan-**electricians**.com/ ▾
1 Hour Service - Free Estimates.
Lowest Rates In New York City.

Find a Local Electrician
electricians.networx.com/ ▾
4.2 ★★★★ rating for networx.com
Licensed, Professional Electricians.
Get Multiple Free Quotes Instantly!

Newark Electrician
www.atlaselectric.co/ ▾
1 hr Response- Servicing NJ Only
$75 diagnostic fee- 24 hr / 7day

OBrien Electric
www.obrien**electrical**.com/ ▾
Residential / Commercial
service@obrienelectrical.com

Local House Painters
www.ozzyspainting.com/HousePainter ▾
Exterior House Painter Contractor
Clean, Professional House Painters
📍 65 Travelo Drive, Wayne, NJ
5.0 ★★★★★ 39 reviews

Electricians Near You
www.**electrical**repairmen.com/ ▾
Find Affordable Electricians Near
You. Enter Your Zip & Search Now!

Call an Electrician Now
www.call-a-pro.com/**electrician** ▾
Need an Electrician for Any Issue?
Call for an Electrician 24/7.

See your ad here ›

Does it Really Matter if You Have a Google Plus Page?

We purposely chose the top listing on the Google 3-pack to see what this company has done well and what they could do better.

You may be thinking, "Why should I do more if I already have the number one listing for Electrician Newark New Jersey?" The answer is very simple.

In competitive markets for service area businesses, other companies may decide to get more aggressive with their efforts and try to overtake the first three spots on the Google 3-pack.

It makes sense, right?

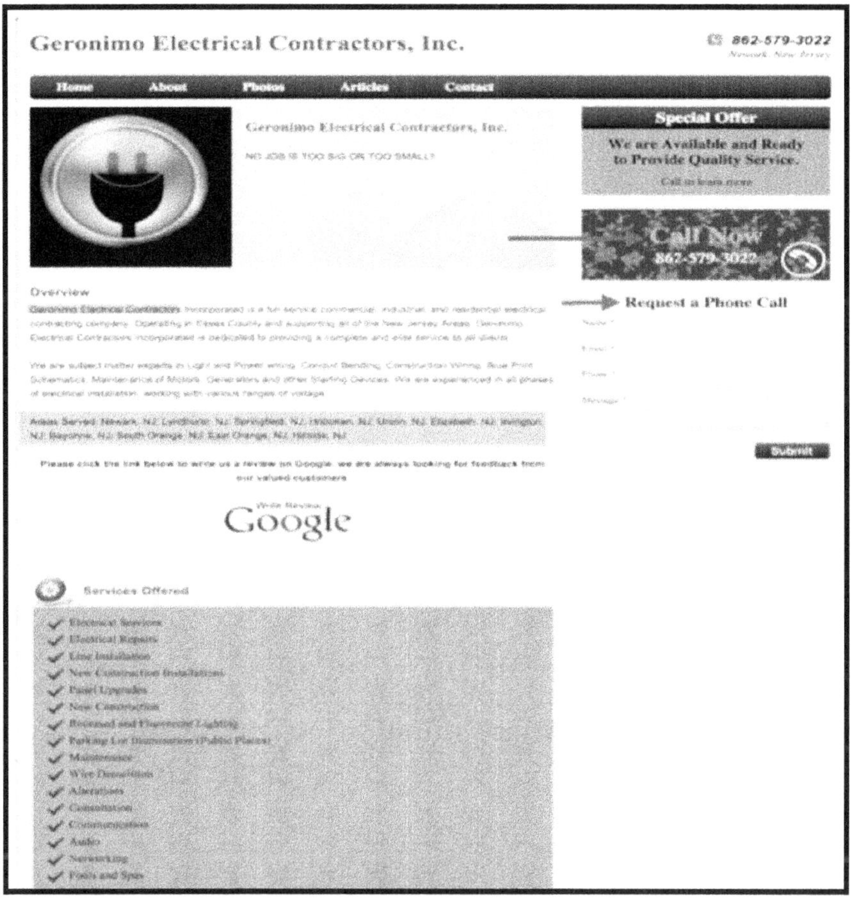

This electrical contractor has a straightforward homepage. The focus is on calling them. They also start the first paragraph with their company name.

They list the services they offer and "below the fold" (not seen here), they have more than 500 words of content. Remember, Google expects you to have a reasonable amount of content and they've done it here.

Okay, so what does this have to do with getting listed in the number one position in the Google 3-pack? Did they get there because they have a great social media presence? Let's take a look at this.

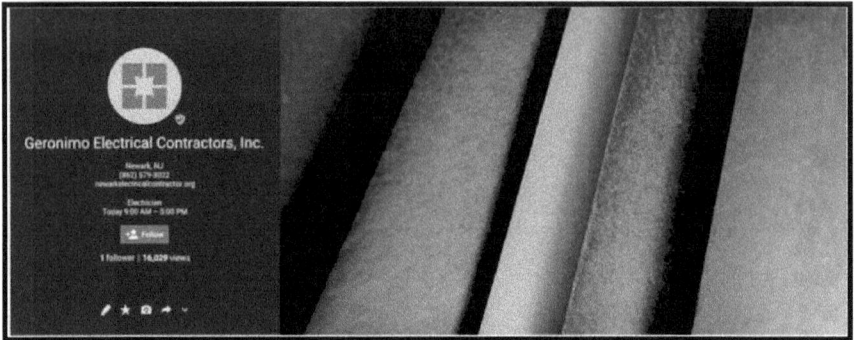

This company signed up for Google Plus, but it hasn't done anything to enhance its listing. This will be one of the algorithms that could knock this company out of the top spot in the Google 3-pack.

This company doesn't appear to have a Facebook page or a Twitter page. Does it make sense for a company like this to even bother with social media sites to enhance its business?

Of Course it Does if You Want to be #1

Sooner or later a company with deep pockets will want to get FREE advertising like this company is getting. When we do a search in the Google Keyword Planner (Newark), we get the following result for "electrician":

Search terms		Avg. monthly searches	Competition	Suggested bid
electrician		90	High	$15.52

The figure in this image is the number of searches that occurs for the word "plumber." For service area businesses, the average sale may be $500. Since this business is number one in the Google 3-pack, it's very likely that they'll get a high percentage of those clicks.

Free clicks beat AdWords clicks any day. So maintaining a top three position in the Google 3-pack is essential for any local business. And this isn't always an easy task in competitive markets.

You achieve authority by making your website SEO friendly and having great content on your site. You also gain authority by the social signals you put out.

If you would like more information on our premium services and "Done-for-You" services please visit us at www.localbusinessassociates.com/services

When you look at what Lou Malnati's Pizza puts out compared to the electrical contractor in Newark, which one would you say did a better job setting themselves up for success in the long run?

Do You Feel Lucky, Punk?

We have to make a point very clear here. Sometimes you get lucky and things go your way. But don't think for one second that luck will keep going your way.

Too many businesses want that number one ranking in Google's 3-pack, and they will eventually figure out what they need to do. Be proactive and continue adding content to your site and to your social media pages like Google Plus, Facebook, Twitter and YouTube.

If you would like more information on our premium services and "Done-for-You" services please visit us at www.localbusinessassociates.com/services

Why Video Marketing Matters

Certain concepts will help you get your videos, articles and web pages ranked at the top of the search engines. The major search engines require metadata descriptions to categorize and rank your content. By following their rules, your content can be ranked on page one.

Why is all of this so important, you may ask? Traffic is the lifeblood of your business. If customers can't find you, how are you going to be successful? The simple answer is to follow the guidelines the major search engines like Google and YouTube require of you.

Start with the keyword research first. Using the right keywords is the metric that matters most for ranking your videos, articles and web pages. Please don't gloss over this concept because it will make all the difference in the world for your success or failure.

Increase Your Online Visibility

Video marketing is designed to help you increase your visibility online and grow your traffic so you can have meaningful relationships with your customers. As much as we'd like to offer you a push-button approach, there isn't one and there will never be one!

Become the expert or have your assistants learn this information and turn it into greater success. Video marketing is taking over as the new medium for marketing success, and you can't afford not to be part of this marketing revolution.

So what's with all the commotion about video marketing?

Oh Yeah, YouTube is a Big Deal

YouTube is the second largest search engine in the world behind Google. Google and YouTube account for approximately 68% of all searches on the Internet.

This alone is reason enough to jump on the bandwagon. But it isn't the only reason. YouTube is a FREE medium for anyone to upload content.

At the beginning of 2013, YouTube introduced a brand new feature to its website. YouTube channel owners now have the ability to add FREE clickable links directly to their videos.

You may be wondering what these clickable links mean? If you link your YouTube channel to an "associated website," you can add links directly in your videos that allow you to send viewers to a squeeze page or landing page.

For now, this service is FREE. The only thing you have to do is allow YouTube to put an advertisement at the beginning of your video. Hopefully, YouTube won't start charging you for this service.

If you're beginning in marketing, you may have noticed the sheer numbers of videos that are shown all over the Internet. More and more people are looking to YouTube to find answers to their problems and questions.

If you would like more information on our premium services and "Done-for-You" services please visit us at www.localbusinessassociates.com/services

Answer Questions Until You Run out of Questions

If you have the ability to provide answers to your viewers' problems and questions, you can start building an audience. This is particularly important if you have little or no money in your budget for marketing.

First and foremost, your videos don't have to be Hollywood quality. For local businesses, it's all about gaining trust and answering your customers' questions.

We're confident you could answer hundreds of questions you've gotten from your customers. Each one of these questions should be made into a 90-120 second video.

Everything we've done for local businesses has been spawned from the work we've done at VideoMarketingScholars.com. This has been tested and tested and tested to make sure it would translate into what works for local businesses.

Google and YouTube reward businesses of any kind if they follow their game plan. Their game plan means you provide the user with the best experience possible. After all, Google is a website and it doesn't want its reputation to be damaged.

What Should Your Videos Include?

➢ Answer a specific question your customer has

➢ Focus on one question in your video

➢ State the problem at the very beginning of the video

➢ Offer 3-10 solutions

➢ Tell your customer to go to your website for more information

➢ Keep the video between 90-120 seconds

Your videos will be broken down into two types of videos:

➢ Frequently Asked Questions (FAQs)

➢ Should Asked Questions (SAQs)

FAQs are the type of questions you get the most such as, "How much does it cost." These types of questions are easy to answer and they need to be turned into videos.

SAQs are the type of questions that will put you above your competition. You know as a local business owner that the thing that separates you from the big box stores is customer service.

Your customers want to trust you and they want to know that you'll provide them with the best solutions. And sometimes price isn't going to be the only determinant a customer will use to buy from you.

Mitch Meyerson said the following in his book, "Success Secrets of the Online Marketing Superstars":

"People today have come to expect to find information about any product, service, company, individual, cause or challenge they face by simply turning to the search engine of their choice. So if they're not finding content that you've produced, there's a pretty good chance you won't be worthy of their trust. Which brings us to the two most important categories when it comes to content strategy: building trust and educating your customer."

Customers prefer video to any other form of research. Video also answers the two most important questions

Mitch Meyerson outlines in his book, building trust and educating your customer.

Building Trust is the Ticket

Before someone even walks in through your front door, it's very likely that they've done some research on you and your business. They may have found you through word of mouth or because of where you're located.

But you want that person to know you through the videos you create even before they visit your business. This builds a trust factor instantly because you've been answering their questions with video.

In the simplest terms, here's what your video should include in 90-120 seconds:

➢ Answer a specific question your customer has

➢ Focus on one question in your video

➢ State the problem at the very beginning of the video

➢ Offer 3-10 solutions

➢ Tell your customer to go to your website for more information

Why Do We Say 90-120 Seconds?

YouTube analytics will be your guide here. You'll see a considerable drop-off of viewership very quickly at a certain point. Here's an example of the YouTube Analytics you have access to when you sign up for a YouTube channel:

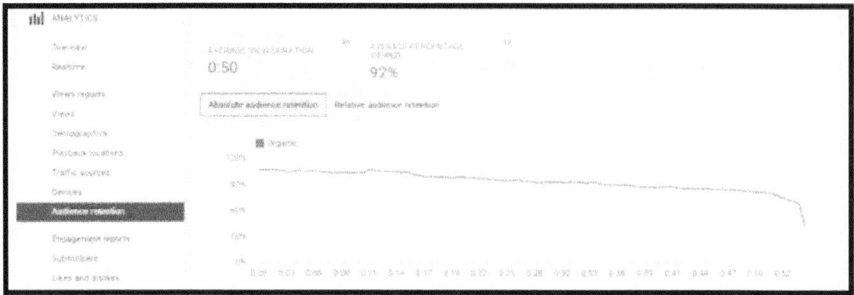

Now let's talk details because we're asking you to do no less than 100 videos for your YouTube channel.

We'll use the analogy of points of interest in a particular state. So you're getting ready to visit Wyoming and you want to find points of interest.

Yellowstone National Park was mentioned seven times in this search occurring above the fold. The point is if you say something often enough a pattern will begin to form.

Your local business may not be as widely recognized as Yellowstone National Park, but you're also not competing on such a large scale. Your goal is to get recognized more often than your local competitor, and YouTube provides you with the perfect medium to do that.

Saturate Your Local Market with Videos

When you create 100 plus videos, you begin saturating the local marketing with your message. It doesn't cost you anything except your time and effort (just like car dealership commercials on TV).

We know your time and effort is just as important as the money you spend on marketing your local business, so you can stop laughing now. 100+ videos is a very achievable number to shoot for...

There's no doubt it will take you some time to refine your message and get comfortable saying the right things to your customer, but you don't have to do a Hollywood production. Get it?

We get asked this question all the time. Why should I do 100 videos? The easy answer is you'll get found more often on YouTube and Google since:

➤ Creating more videos means YouTube will start categorizing more of your videos in the same location or market

➤ Creating more videos means you'll begin to dominate a niche

➤ Creating more videos means you'll begin to create more authority for your brand and your channel

➤ Creating more videos means you'll get ranked higher than a video or a channel that has many more views but fewer videos

➤ Creating more videos means more people will find your clickable links to your squeeze pages or landing pages

Your Message is Your Word

Your message is the most important thing you can do on a YouTube video. We've given you the points you need to have in your 90-120 second videos to get people to go over to your website or landing page.

If you would like more information on our premium services and "Done-for-You" services please visit us at www.localbusinessassociates.com/services

Equally as important in this whole strategy is how to get your videos ranked high on page one of the major search engines like Google and YouTube.

You could have the greatest video ever made, but if people can't find it because it's buried on page 50 of Google, you won't have any way of getting people over to your website.

In fact, if you aren't in the top five listings of page one of Google, there's a very slim chance that anyone will click on your link whether it's a video or a post.

Write Good Titles, Okay?

Your video titles will either attract viewers or turn them off. Your titles need to be compelling. The two most compelling title formats are:

Asking a question as if you were having a conversation with someone

Providing tips and lists people could be doing to solve their problem or dilemma

Here are a few examples; you decide which ones pique your interest:

➢ Lose Weight For The Holidays

➢ Is Belly Fat Ruining Your Sex Life?

➢ 10 Flat Belly Secrets

➢ Strip Away Fat

➢ Melt Your Fat

By the way, these titles came from covers of Men's Health Magazine.

We've talked about keywords derived from the Google Keyword Planner and semantic text equivalents. The key to good titles is to be compelling and keep your titles under 60 characters (with spaces).

Google recently completed a major algorithm change and decided that asking questions as if you were in a conversation with someone sitting across the table from you was more relevant to finding the answers you were searching for.

Rule 1: Titles should be framed as a question

Rule 2: Titles should be compelling

Rule 3: Titles should have a keyword (phrase)

Rule 4: Titles shouldn't have more than 60 characters with spaces

Clogged Toilets, Holy Crap!

Let's take a look at how you should construct your title with an example. We'll start by looking for a keyword phrase in the Google Keyword Planner.

Search terms	Avg. monthly searches	Competition	Suggested bid
clogged toilet	9,900	Medium	$6.27

We chose "clogged toilet" from the Google Keyword Planner and we'll formulate a title around this keyword phrase.

We hear you laughing, but here's the rationale for choosing this term if you're a plumber. People may think they can solve the problem themselves. Maybe they can or maybe they can't.

Let's say they watch your video that's at the top of page one on Google and they can't fix the problem. Your solution is to have them call you. You've earned some credibility by helping them for free, but now they need a plumber. Who do you think they're going to call?

So here goes...

How Do You Unclog A Clogged Toilet | Applewood Plumbing

This title starts with a question and it has 55 characters with spaces. It also has the name of the business in the title. It worked out fine here, but there's something you need to know regarding the construction of your title. We'll discuss this in a second.

If you're using Microsoft Word, go to the bottom of the Word document and click on "Words." Here's what this looks like for this example:

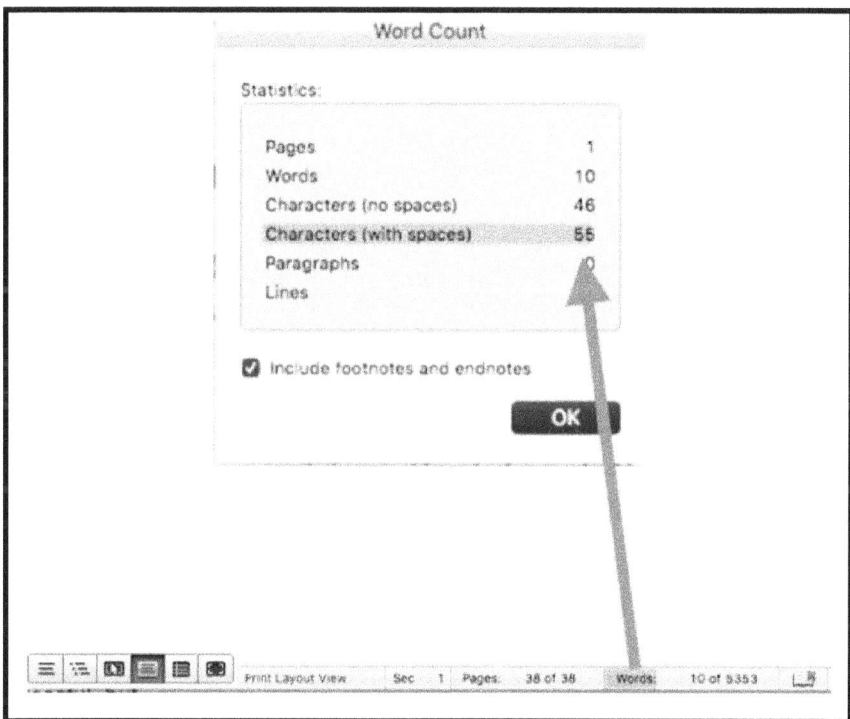

Ranking Rules of Engagement

Before we go any further, it's important to understand that ranking your videos on page one of Google must follow several rules.

The first rule is that if you see a local map and a Google 3-pack on page one, it may be very difficult to get your video in the first five positions on page one of Google.

We chose Applewood Plumbing in this example, but if we were to choose "Plumbers In Denver" the results would look entirely different.

Let's take a look at both examples on Google so it makes more sense to you:

If you would like more information on our premium services and "Done-for-You" services please visit us at www.localbusinessassociates.com/services

You'll notice that no Google Map or Google 3-pack is associated with the search "How do you unclog a clogged toilet | Applewood Plumbing."

This is exactly what we want to see. Now let's take a look at it as if you were looking for a plumber in Denver using the keyword phrase "Plumber in Denver."

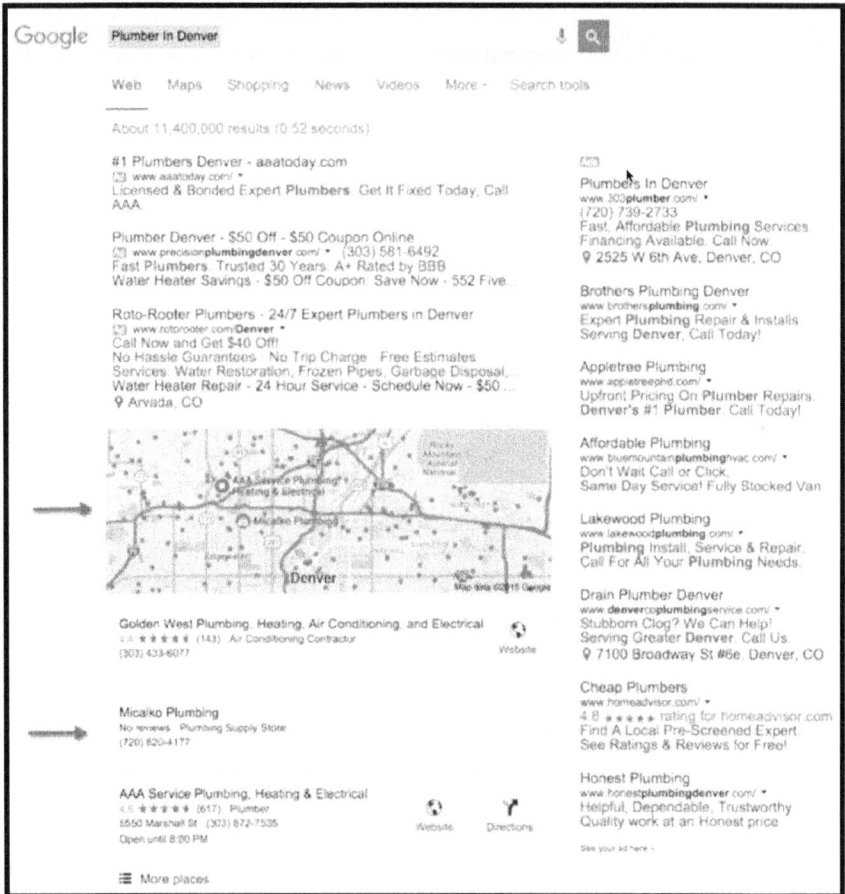

We know what you're thinking. Why not try to get your video ranked on the page with the keyword phrase, "Plumber in Denver?" You can try and try and try, but you'll most likely not get your video ranked on page one of Google.

Any time you see the Google Map and Google 3-pack, you'll have great difficulty getting your videos ranked. So the best plan of action is to create videos to answer questions and get them ranked on page one by asking a question.

If you would like more information on our premium services and "Done-for-You" services please visit us at www.localbusinessassociates.com/services

Always copy and paste your title into a Google search first and make sure it doesn't generate the Google Map and Google 3-pack before you decide on the title.

Please don't get confused with videos and your website. Videos are meant to answer questions you routinely get from your customers because they help you build trust and authority.

Plus, YouTube is considered a social media site, so you are building social authority as well.

We've discussed keywords already, but it's important to use 10-15 keywords in the description.

When you begin to upload a video to YouTube, you'll have to find the video file on your computer to upload. Once you click on the upload button, you can enter your keywords and a description.

YouTube refers to keywords as "tags," so don't get confused with the terminology. It may seem like a pain in the ass to find 10-15 keywords every time you create a video, but it will give you FREE advertising if you do it correctly.

There will be considerable over-lap in the keywords you use for each video and that's okay. This helps you dominate your market because the search engines keep seeing a pattern in your content.

So how do you justify using 10-15 keywords?

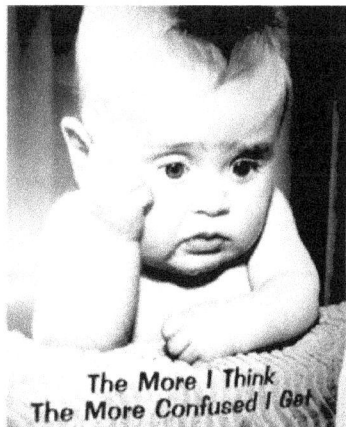

The More I Think
The More Confused I Get

The Big Mistake

The biggest mistake 99% of people make when putting videos on YouTube is not entering their keywords or description in the space provided for both items.

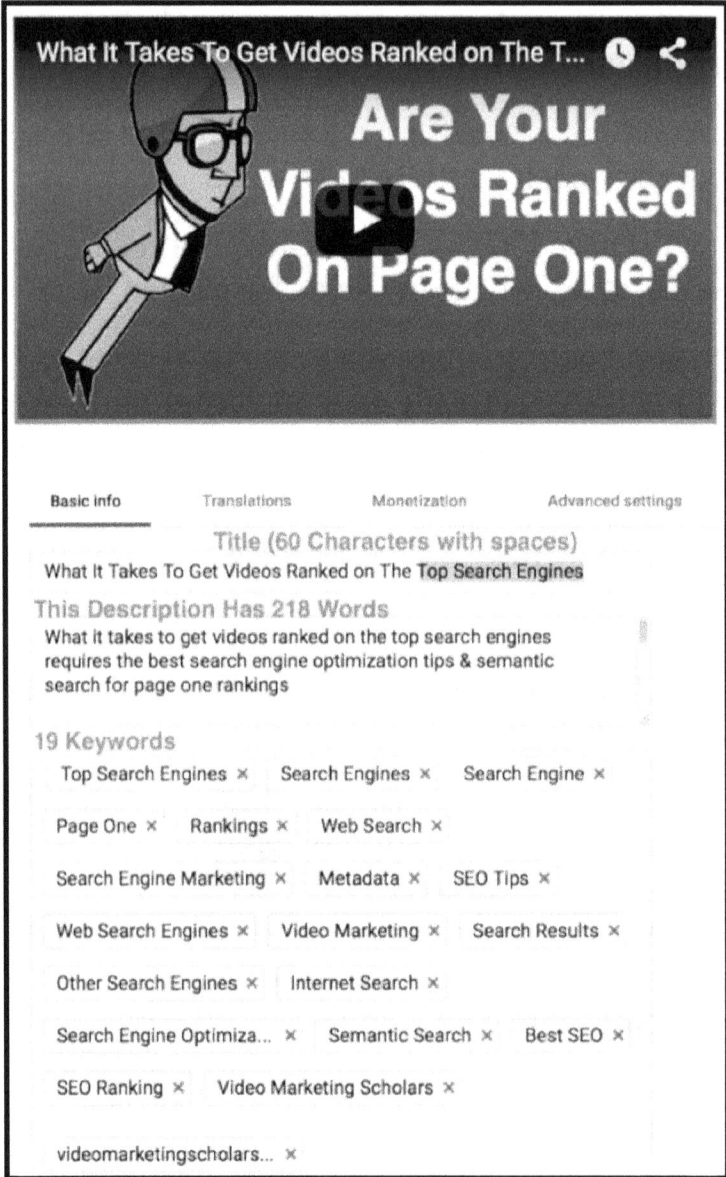

Here's the full 218-word description so you can see what it contains.

What it takes to get videos ranked on the top search engines requires the best search engine optimization tips & semantic search for page one rankings

When someone does a web search on Google or other search engines, video thumbnails will generally catch that viewer's attention when they see the search results on page one

The best SEO results come from using the right meta-data (titles, descriptions, keywords)

In order to achieve a top spot in Internet search results, you may also have to consider how a viewer will do semantic search to find what they're looking for

Competition for the top spots on page one demand that you use search engine marketing strategies that include semantic search strategies as well as keyword research

At Video Marketing Scholars (videomarketingscholars.com), we provide you with the best SEO tips so you can get your videos ranked on page one on all the web search engines

Keep in mind that you could have the greatest video in the world, but if you're not using the right metadata, your video marketing efforts won't get you anywhere

Your ultimate goal is to be found everywhere so people consume your content. At http://VideoMarketingSchol-ars.com we offer a free mini-course. Please sign up for it and get your videos and articles ranked number one.

The description, title and keywords will result in page one top rankings on Google if you follow the plan we lay out here. If you decide to skip our recommendations, you may not have the success you expect. Here's the result for this video:

Proof of Concept

How To **Promote Your Business** By Making Videos To Answer Questions

Web   Videos   News   Shopping   Images   More ▾   Search tools

About 46,000,000 results (0.37 seconds)

How To Promote Your Business By Making Videos To ...
www.youtube.com/watch?v=6AXTvpFcagU
Jan 21, 2015 - Uploaded by Video Marketing Scholars
How to promote your business by making videos to answer
questions customers is easy. Learn how to build ...

▶ 3:00

Why Do Webinars And **Email Marketing** Lead to More Money

Web   News   Videos   Images   Shopping   More ▾   Search tools

About 8,950,000 results (0.39 seconds)

Why Do Webinars And Email Marketing Lead to More Money
https://www.youtube.com/watch?v=5eWYWTzqdaA
Mar 2, 2015 - Uploaded by Video Marketing Scholars
Why do webinars and email marketing lead to more money?
Holding a live meeting with web conferencing ...

▶ 2:27

How To **Increase Leads** And **Web Traffic** Using **Video Marketing**

Web   News   Images   Videos   Shopping   More ▾   Search tools

About 7,570,000 results (0.40 seconds)

How To Increase Leads And Web Traffic Using Video ...
https://www.youtube.com/watch?v=hgHC09VCADE
Jan 20, 2015 - Uploaded by Video Marketing Scholars
How to increase leads and web traffic using video marketing is
needed to get customers and leads for email ...

▶ 3:09

If you would like more information on our premium services and "Done-for-You" services please visit us at www.localbusinessassociates.com/services

Do You Need SEO Services To Win At Search Engine Optimization

Web   News   Videos   Images   Shopping   More ▾   Search tools

About 4,310,000 results (0.85 seconds)

Do You Need SEO Services To Win At Search Engine ...
https://www.youtube.com/watch?v=AbtW5dRhrVA
Jan 10, 2015 - Uploaded by Video Marketing Scholars
Do you need SEO services to win at search engine
▶ 2:59   optimization? If you are doing video marketing or article ...

Can video marketing help your local business achieve success

Web   News   Images   Videos   Shopping   More ▾   Search tools

About 13,600,000 results (0.49 seconds)

Can Video Marketing Help Your Local Business Achieve ...
https://www.youtube.com/watch?v=iFWu9_he0ho
Sep 22, 2015 - Uploaded by Local Business Associates
Can Video Marketing Help Your Local Business Achieve
▶ 2:47   Success ... promote your website through Local SEO ...

Video Marketing Scholars - YouTube
https://www.youtube.com/user/VideoMarketingStud ▾
VMS helps Internet marketers and business owners get ranked on Page 1 of Google and
... Can video marketing help your local business achieve success?
You've visited this page 3 times. Last visit: 3/8/15

How Does Video Marketing Help Grow Local Businesses ...
https://www.youtube.com/watch?v=v0Tdsnb7VUc
Sep 14, 2015 - Uploaded by Local Business Associates
How Does Video Marketing Help Grow Local Businesses ... Can
▶ 3:05   Your Local Business Get Free Advertising ...

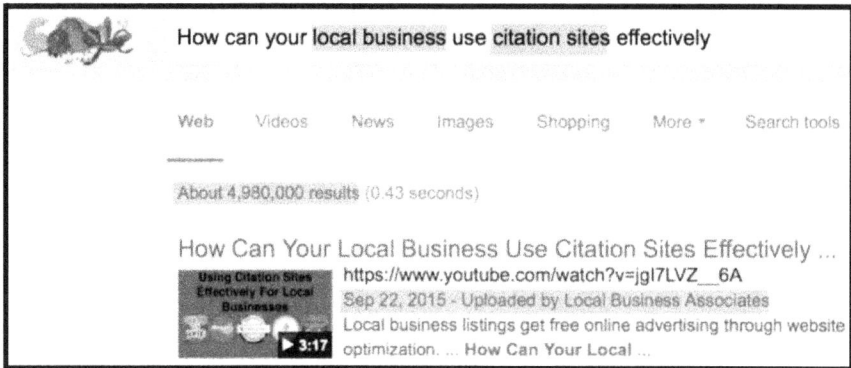

What Should Your Description Be?

This may sound a little crazy, but the first 60 characters of your description should be your title. You can see on all the examples we've shown here that the title is repeated.

The first 150 characters of the description should include the title (first 60 characters) and the remaining 90 characters should include several keywords.

This strategy has worked for the past five years because we've followed the guidelines Google and YouTube want you to follow. Too often, people think they can game the system, but that rarely works over time.

Does it matter if you do a talking head video or a slide presentation?

No, your message is much more important that the format you use. If you don't want to get in front of the camera, use PowerPoint or Keynote.

It will take you some time to get comfortable shooting a video or doing the voiceover for your slide presentation, but it will make a big difference in the long run.

Custom Thumbnails are Your Secret Weapon

The last thing we'll cover here are custom thumbnails. You saw in the examples we showed previously that YouTube allows you to upload custom thumbnails.

Why should you create custom thumbnails?

When people are searching for information on Google or YouTube, they're attracted to the thumbnail and if it looks interesting to them, they'll click on the link.

That's exactly what we want them to do. This is how you get traffic to your website. Here are the dimensions you can use for your thumbnails.

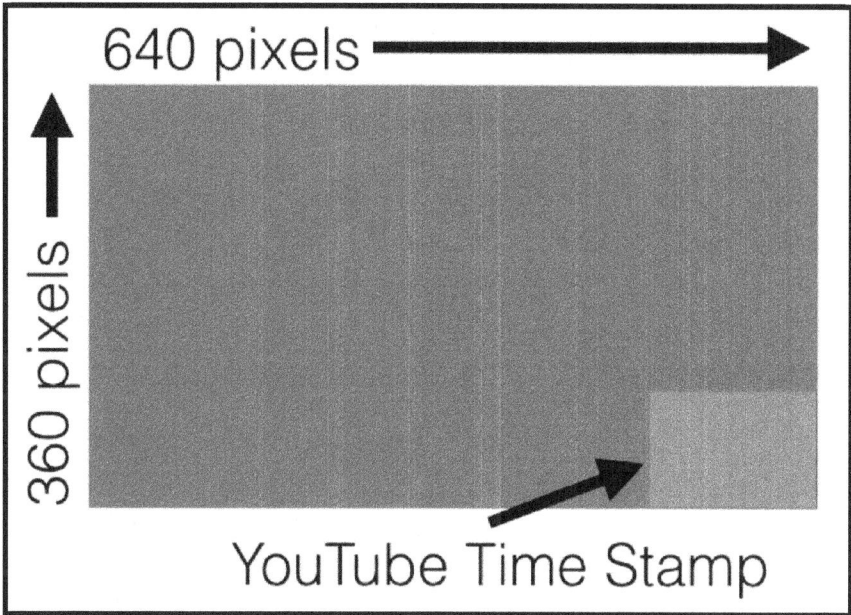

If you aren't working with pixels, you can use a 16:9 ratio. YouTube will allow any variation of a 16:9 ratio.

Keep in mind that thumbnails are small, but you want your images and text to be as big as you can make them without encroaching on the time stamp in the bottom right corner of the thumbnail.

Also, don't be afraid to use really bright colors for your backgrounds and crazy images. People will notice this very easily when all the other listings on page one are just text.

One last thing we want to mention. Creating hundreds of videos should be your goal because you will get FREE traffic to your website. Think about the money you spend on local advertising. If it isn't working effectively, you'll find that video marketing will.

On-Page Search Engine Optimization

On-page SEO is the lifeblood of every page or post on your website. We've already talked about keywords and semantic text and now we'll discuss how you implement this strategy.

Undoubtedly, you've received hundreds of calls from marketers saying they're SEO experts and they can get your website ranked high on the search engines.

Some of these companies probably do a good job and you may decide to hire them. Google has specific algorithms to determine how websites and web pages are ranked.

This information is secret proprietary information that Google will never share with the public. However, SEO experts can surmise many of the algorithms based on rankings.

Google's main priority is to provide users with the best search experience, and they'll drop your rankings if you're trying to fool the viewers.

Let's get started so that you can do this yourself or find a company that truly understands what it takes to really help you get better ranking.

Brand Your Business

You're a local business owner and your number one priority should be to brand your business. You can't mention your business often enough on your website.

Using pronouns is acceptable, but using your business name is always the way to go. Here's an example of a business that uses its business name to its benefit:

NYC Plumbers: Plumbing Service in New York City

Serving the New York Metropolitan Area

Imagine your plumbers rolling out a red carpet, covering their work boots with booties, wearing ID badges, and crisp, clean uniforms.

Welcome to Hub Plumbing & Mechanical of New York City, where we are ready to roll out our Red Carpet Service at YOUR convenience, 24 hours a day, 7 days a week, 365 days a year.

Hub Plumbing & Mechanical was recently featured in a new book entitled The Celebrity Experience where Hub Plumbing & Mechanicals Red Carpet Service was cited as an example of how its possible to create faithful lifelong customers by showering them with treatment usually reserved for celebrities

Our NYC Plumbers ← This is hyper-linked text

Our NYC Plumbing Company is a trusted New York plumbing company name, known for quality, professional NYC plumbers and superior work. We offer prompt expert plumbing service from our **Plumbers in NYC** for your home or business, with available same day and emergency plumbing repairs.

Local Business Associates like what they did here on their homepage. They mentioned their name three times. We wouldn't have had a problem if they mentioned it a fourth time instead of using "NYC Plumbing Company," but "plumbing company" is a keyword phrase and it's hyperlinked.

Hyperlinked text means that when you click on it, it will lead to another page on your website or someone else's website or post.

Unfortunately, this link isn't working and that's a strike against them as far as Google is concerned. So the lesson is, when you use hyperlinks make sure they lead to something.

Why Hyperlink?

If you're wondering why you'd link to someone else's website or post, here's why. It allows you to do the research instantly for your viewer.

For example, you own a high-end bakery and maybe you were trained at a prestigious culinary school in France. You could hyperlink text that gives information to your viewers where you were trained.

This doesn't hurt your business, but it enhances your reputation because you've done some research for your viewers about your expertise. This certainly would appeal to high-end customers.

Let's look at another example that will allow viewers to decide if they want to do business with you.

Heating and air conditioning companies use different manufacturers to buy products for customers. A simple hyperlinked text to one of the manufacturers saves viewers the time to find products they may be interested in.

Here's an example of this hyperlinked text...

AIR CONDITIONERS

Brennan offers air conditioners from only top manufacturers such as Lennox. ⬅———

To be the leader in the industry, we understand that every customer and application is unique, and we must have a wide array of options to completely satisfy every customer. Brennan Heating & Air Conditioning offers repair and installation of air conditioners in Seattle and throughout the Puget Sound region.

This hyperlinked text then opens to this page...

LENNOX

Vision + Innovation = One hundred plus years of innovation.

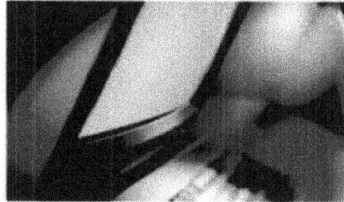

Foundation for Success

In 1895, Dave Lennox single-handedly elevated the standard of American living by pioneering the riveted-steel furnace. Working from his machine shop in Marshalltown, Iowa, Dave Lennox began building the first Lennox® furnaces and joined legendary inventors like Bell and Edison in laying the foundation for the 20th century.

Focus on Innovation

As Dave Lennox paved the way for modern home comfort, he put together a solid formula for long-term success. At the heart of this formula is a focus on innovation, hard work and sound business practices. It is this vision that has kept Lennox at the forefront of the HVAC industry for more than 100 years.

Finest Products Available

Today, the Lennox name is recognized throughout the world for quality home comfort. So when you see the Lennox label, you can count on exceptional performance and reliability. And when you see the Dave Lennox signature, you know you're getting the finest, most innovative heating, cooling and indoor air quality products available.

Here's a suggestion if you don't think you have the time to do this yourself. Call the local community college, college or university in your area and see if students are looking for writing jobs.

You can tell them what you want and you can tell them to hyperlink text leading back to other pages on your website and to outside website sources.

What the Heck is an ALT Tag?

Okay, now let's look at the images you use on your web pages. Every image you use should be tagged with what is called an "ALT tag."

The reason you need to do this is because the search engines like Google, Bing and Yahoo can't interpret the image or photo unless you assign an ALT tag to it.

ALT tag is known as alternate text and it's important that you label everything on your website with this tag.

If you're working with a webmaster, this individual should know how to do it. So what should you call the image or photo?

➢ Your business name

➢ Keywords you want to get found for

➢ Specials or offers you plan to give to your customers

Here's what a basic ALT tag looks like:

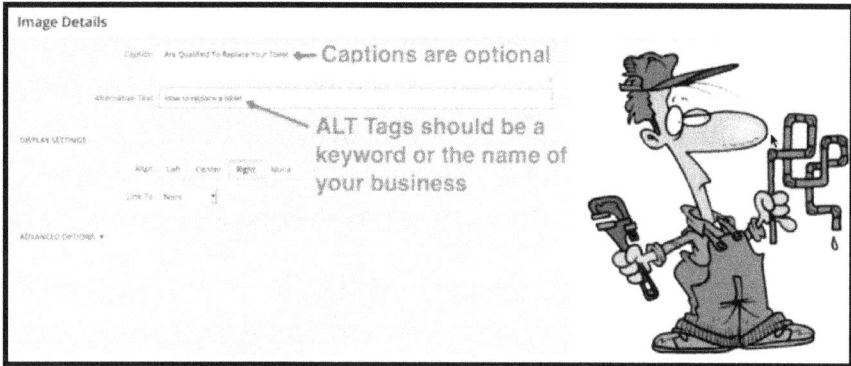

Now we'll look at several more features of on-page SEO that you should be doing all the time:

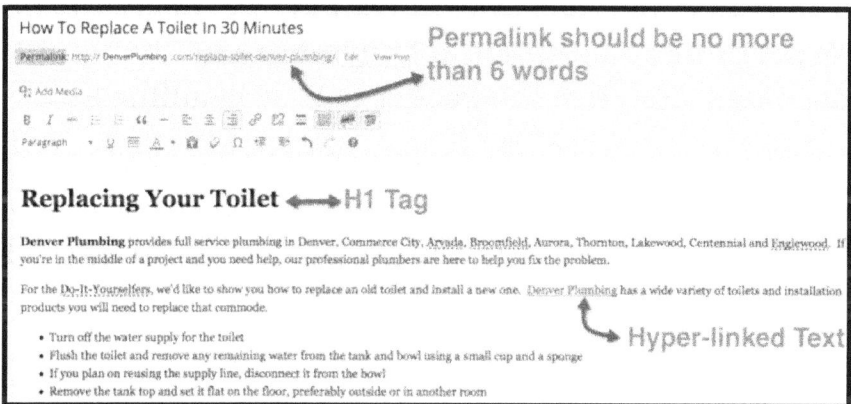

Depending on the platform you use for your website, you should be able to add a permalink to every web page and every post you create.

Is a Permalink Worth it?

The permalink is an essential piece of information for the search engines to identify a particular page or post. You should be using keywords and your business name or city. In the example above, there are four words in the permalink, "replace-toilet-denver-plumbing."

Don't worry about using words like is, the, a, and or it. Pick out the most important words as we've done here. If you don't add your own permalink, you'll just see a series of numbers, letter and symbols. Make sure you use hyphens after each word!

Header Tags are Your Headlines

The next component we'll look at is the header tags. While this isn't as important anymore, you should still use them. Think of the header tags as headlines.

The H1 tag is the main headline and you should use some variation of your main keyword (semantic text works great here). Each successive header tag would be H2, H3 and H4.

These little on-page SEO tactics will amount to better rankings and that's exactly what you should be aiming for.

We also showed you an example of hyperlinked text. This is another component you shouldn't ignore. Linking other pages from your website or linking to outside sources helps your ranking too. The New York Times does this all the time.

On-Page SEO Essentials

Website platforms should allow you to add your own SEO components like your title, keywords and description. This is a little different than YouTube because your description will only be about 150 characters with spaces.

Your title still should stay less than 60 characters with spaces and you should have 10-15 keywords if your platform allows it. Here's an example of a WordPress. org SEO form:

How To Replace A Toilet in 30 Min

http://www.DenverPlumbing.com/replacing-toilet-Denver-Plumbing
How to replace your toilet in 30 minutes. With a few hand tools switching out your commode is
easy. Call Denver Plumbing 1-303-555-1212 for a plumber

(This is how your listing will look like on Google)

(?) Title   How To Replace A Toilet in 30 Min **(45 Characters with spaces)**

(?) Description   How to replace your toilet in 30 minutes. With a few hand tools switching out your
commode is easy. Call Denver Plumbing 1-303-555-1212 for a plumber

149 characters. Most search engines use a maximum of 160 chars for the description.

(?) Keywords (comma separated)   Replace A Toilet, Plumber In Denver, Denver Plumber, Plumber, Plumbing Company Denve

Too many people don't add this information, and it makes it harder for the search engines to categorize your information properly. Don't be one of those people because it will help you beat your competition!

With regards to using keywords, it isn't about stuffing as many keywords as you can onto one page. The key is to use your main keyword a few times throughout your pages or posts.

If you write 500 words or more, you won't have any problems using 10 keywords or semantic text without it looking like you're "keyword stuffing."

The frequency of your main keyword should be limited to no more than 3-4 times per 500 words. Intersperse the remaining keywords 1-2 times only. Google and the other search engines will know how to categorize your information.

Proximity is also a very important on-page SEO tactic. Proximity means that you use a keyword or semantic text close to your business name or city and state.

Here's an example of proximity for Google Planner Keywords and semantic text.

On-page SEO can seem like a daunting task, but if you apply a few tactics consistently, you'll do very well compared to your competitors.

The biggest thing you need to know about expanding your business is to research what people are doing before they come into your business.

Smartphone and tablet use has surpassed laptop and desktop use. This means you need to be on top of your game regardless of how small your business is.

Is Your Website Mobile-Ready?

There are five very good reasons why your website should be mobile ready regardless of the size of your business:

5 Mobile-Optimized Website Benefits

Improved User Experience

➤ When you get texts from someone and you try to open the link and it's gobbledygook, this will kill any chance you have of converting that visitor into a customer. If the user can't easily browse and read the content on your website from their mobile device, they won't come back

➤ Reports show that 60% of mobile users have encountered problems when browsing websites that have led them to abandon the page

Increased Average Time on Site

➤ Time is a precious commodity and it's no different online. You have a limited amount of time to capture a website visitor's attention

➤ Visitors that can navigate your mobile-ready website are more likely to take action and buy goods and services from you

Faster Website Load Speed

➢ Speed is important because a website that isn't mobile optimized will render very slowly on your mobile device or it may not load at all

➢ A mobile-ready website will load quickly because the code is structured in a way that is compatible with mobile devices

➢ Studies show mobile website users will abandon a page if they have to wait more than 6-10 seconds

Improved Mobile SEO

➢ Following Google's rules is the only way to go

➢ Google recommends that webmasters build sites as mobile ready, but if that isn't an option, Google prefers your business make a separate HTML website to serve mobile users, increasing the likelihood that your site will rank better among Google mobile search

Competitive Advantage Over Your Competition

➢ Depending on your business market, there's a good chance many of your competitors don't have a mobile-ready website. We know this is a bad omen because viewers won't stay on a site if it looks bad or doesn't load quickly

This excerpt comes from the Google Webmaster Central Blog:

Webmaster Central Blog

Official news on crawling and indexing sites for the Google index

Finding more mobile-friendly search results

Thursday, February 26, 2015

When it comes to search on mobile devices, users should get the most relevant and timely results, no matter if the information lives on mobile-friendly web pages or apps. As more people use mobile devices to access the Internet, our algorithms have to adapt to these usage patterns. In the past, we've made updates to ensure a site is configured properly and viewable on modern devices. We've made it easier for users to find mobile-friendly web pages and we've introduced App Indexing to surface useful content from apps. Today, we're announcing two important changes to help users discover more mobile-friendly content:

1. More mobile-friendly websites in search results

Starting April 21, we will be expanding our use of mobile friendliness as a ranking signal. This change will affect mobile searches in all languages worldwide and will have a significant impact in our search results. Consequently, users will find it easier to get relevant, high quality search results that are optimized for their devices.

To get help with making a mobile-friendly site, check out our guide to mobile-friendly sites. If you're a webmaster, you can get ready for this change by using the following tools to see how Googlebot views your pages:

➢ If you want to test a few pages, you can use the Mobile-Friendly Test.

➢ If you have a site, you can use your Webmaster Tools account to get a full list of mobile usability issues across your site using the Mobile Usability Report.

2. More relevant app content in search results

Starting today, we'll begin to use information from indexed apps as a factor in ranking for signed-in users who have the app installed. As a result, we may now surface content from indexed apps more prominently in search. To find out how to implement App Indexing, which allows us to surface this information in search results, have a look at our step-by-step guide on the developer site.

If you have questions about either mobile-friendly websites or App Indexing, we're always happy to chat in our Webmaster Help Forum.

Let's take a look at examples of a local website that is mobile-ready and one that isn't.

You'll be able to use the following link to check your website:

https://www.google.com/webmasters/tools/mobile-friendly/

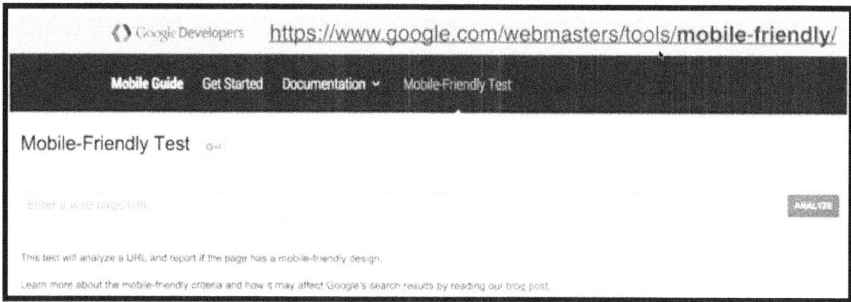

Type your URL into the box and see if your website is mobile ready.

In this example, the plumbing company in Miami IS NOT mobile ready:

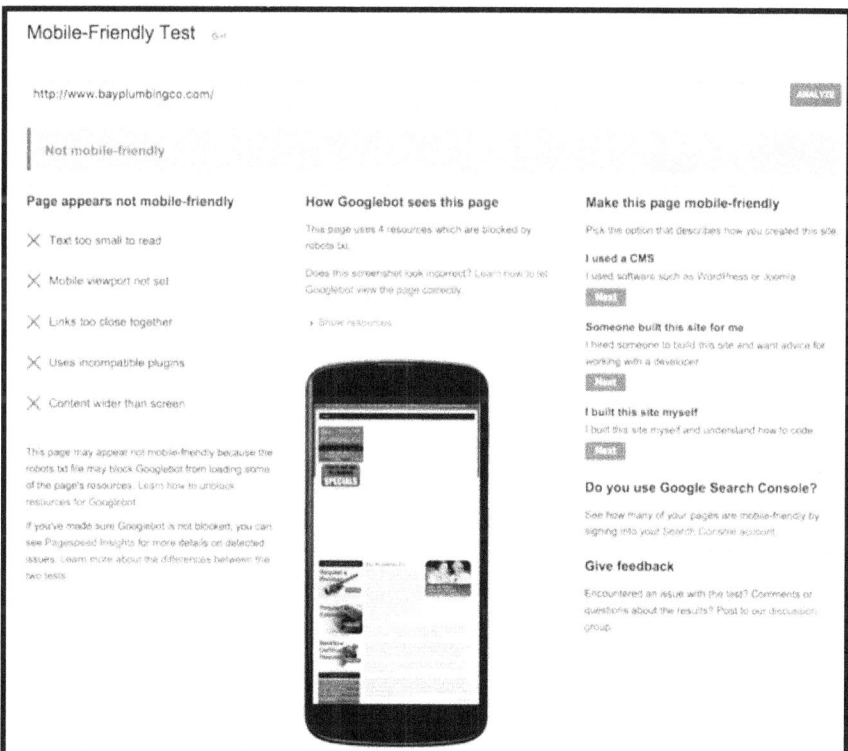

In this example, the plumber in Phoenix has a mobile-ready website:

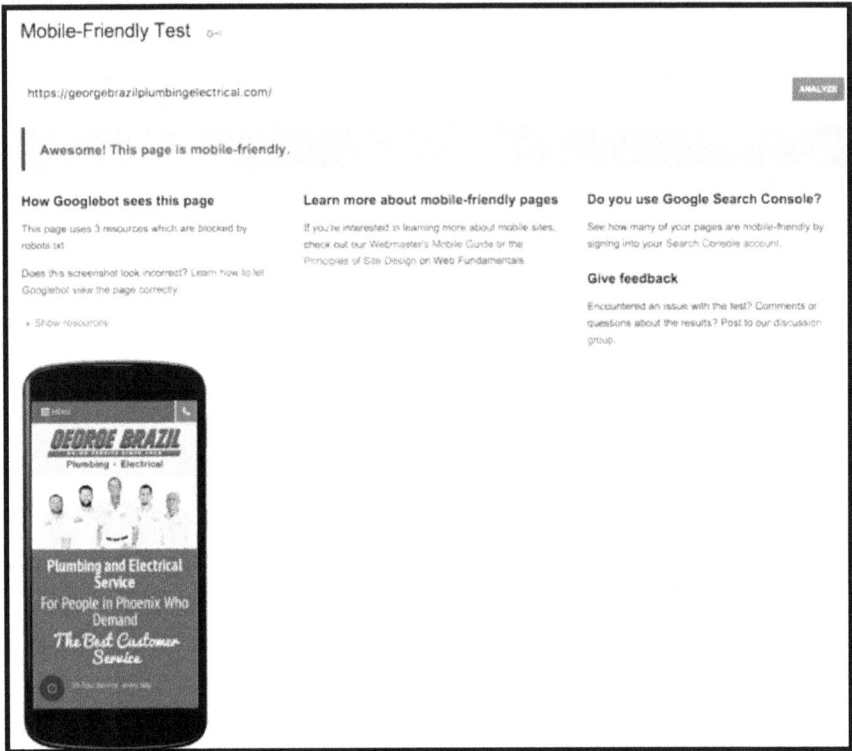

Is This a Nice to Know Fact?

No, this is a crucial part of your website. If you have a WordPress site, it's very easy to use a plugin to make your website mobile ready.

If you have a different platform, you may have to ask your webmaster to help make your website mobile ready.

Based on Google's blog in early 2015, they're going to address mobile readiness in their algorithms. This means you have to take this seriously.

Think About This for a Second...

When you go into any coffee shop, food court or public place you see people searching on their smartphones or tablets.

If these people are searching for services you and your competitors offer, whom are they going to go to if they can't read your information properly?

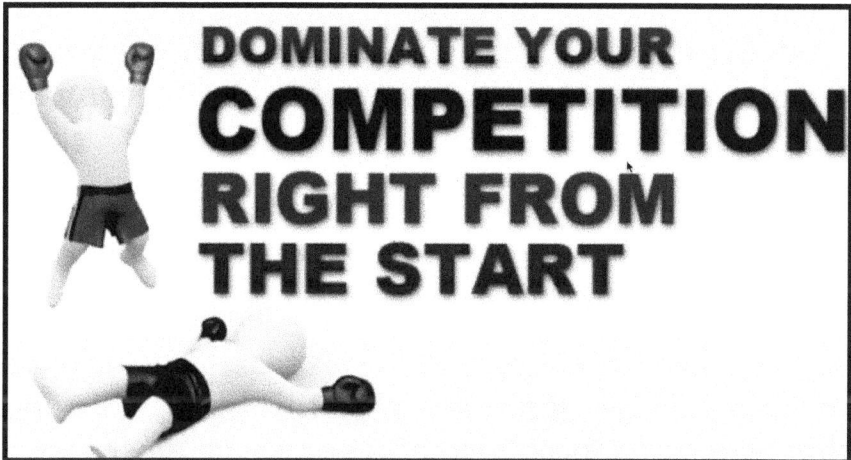

Your local business has to stay current. It may seem painful at first, but take one step at a time and begin making your website ready for any personal device usage.

Conclusion

Running a local business is a monumental task and it only seems to get harder. *Local Business Associates* wants to thank you for reading through the content.

We've provided you with content that will help you grow your business. The **first topic** we covered dealt with having a website that is Google ready.

The Internet is becoming more transparent if you plan on doing business through Google, and that's a very important fact to know. The days of trying to get around Google's rules are OVER!

Verify your website on Google Webmaster Tools and Bing Webmaster Tools. This leads to the transparency Google and Bing expect.

The **second topic** we covered was search engine optimization (SEO). Studies showed this topic is the one that concerned local business owners the most.

SEO does not need to be some abstract monster that will take you down. *Local Business Associates* has provided you with the basics to get started on the right track.

Keep in mind that SEO is not something you do once and then forget. Google, Bing, Yahoo and all the other search engines change the rules frequently, and you need to keep up with them.

The good news though is that you can be relatively safe if you follow the things we have outlined here on SEO.

If you would like more information on our premium services and "Done-for-You" services please visit us at www.localbusinessassociates.com/services

Focus on providing the best user experience you can and you'll be way ahead of your competitors.

The **third topic** we covered was beating the big boys. Google handles local businesses differently than the big boys because your market is local and theirs aren't local.

With that said, there are many things you should copy from them and incorporate into your business (namely blogs, YouTube videos, advertising specials and social media).

Local Business Associates can't say this enough. You can follow the suggestions we're giving you here or you can skip it. But, you can imagine the consequences if your competitors are doing it and you aren't.

The **fourth topic** we covered was why video marketing matters. Video marketing is far and away the most important type of marketing you can do for your business.

Local Business Associates recommends doing videos to accomplish two things. First, build authority and trust with your customers. People will watch your videos and get the sense they know you before they even come into your business.

There's nothing better to build trust with than video marketing.

The second recommendation we give for video marketing is to help solve your customers' problems or dilemmas. Customers love to get answers to their questions, and creating videos for each question you encounter is pure gold.

Viewers love to watch videos and they don't enjoy reading as much, so take advantage of video marketing. Just like anything else, it will take some time to get comfortable with it, but it's worth it for your business.

The **fifth topic** we covered was on-page SEO. On the surface, this seems like a difficult topic, but it isn't. There are few fundamental rules you should follow.

First, use search engine optimization strategies on every page, post, Twitter post, Google Plus post and Facebook post you create.

You'll need to be creative so your titles don't sound too boring. This will help your business immensely.

If you would like more information on our premium services and "Done-for-You" services please visit us at www.localbusinessassociates.com/services

Second, using city names and your business name in the permalinks, titles and H1 tags is very important and it isn't hard to do.

Third, semantic text is becoming more and more important to Google. Google believes people will get a better user experience if they're asking questions as if they were talking to a person across the table.

The **sixth topic** we discussed was having a mobile-ready website. This has become a very important tactic to implement. More and more people are using their mobile devices to search for local businesses and it's imperative that you have a mobile-ready website.

Thank you again for reading through the information *Local Business Associates* has provided you.

If you would like more information on our premium services and "Done-for-You" services please visit us at www.localbusinessassociates.com/services

We have one last thing to ask you and we recommend you do the same on your website and videos.

It's a "Call To Action"...

People will generally respond to your call to action, and you can't be afraid to ask.

Close

We hope this information has been helpful to you and hope that you'll put these steps and strategies into action to improve and increase your business.

If you'd like more information on our premium services and "Done-for-You" services, please visit us at www. LocalBusinessAssociates.com.

"You can't escape the responsibility of tomorrow by evading it today."

About the Authors

Ray Riechert has been an Internet marketer since 2008. After 20 years of corporate life, he chose a franchise opportunity. This gave him the chance to find ways to advertise his business on the Internet. He didn't know it at the time, but his research background helped him build a world-class ranking system for YouTube videos and local businesses that save local businesses money in advertising costs. He is the mad scientist of the team.

Scott Morris has been a serial entrepreneur since being discharged from the USMC in 1980. He started more than 12 successful businesses from scratch before turning his attention to Internet marketing. To hone his skills on the Internet, he joined the most successful Internet marketer of all time, Eben Pagan, and for four years was his senior consultant. While on Eben's team, Scott met Ray Riechert, and together they've

developed some of the most robust and user friendly tools for ranking videos online. Through Local Business Associates, LLC, Scott, Ray, and Jerry deliver all of their combined experience and knowledge so that local business owner can dominate Local Google Search results for their individual businesses, delivering more traffic through their front doors, resulting in more sales.

It's really simple; If you are not #1 in Local Google Search results for what you do, you are invisible to your customers, period.

Jerry Riechert has been an entrepreneur ever since his days as president of the Business School Marketing Club in college. During his corporate days, he was responsible for negotiating mega-million dollar real estate deals. As a result of his negotiating skills, he came on board with Local Business Associates to lead the financial strategies to help local business owners succeed for less. His services bring a powerful force to the company.

Kathy Roberts has been an entrepreneur as far back as she can remember. Even throughout her stay-at-home mothering career, she had many successful businesses to supplement the family income and satisfy her enterprise itch. After developing a course to teach home organization, she dove right into the World Wide Web, converted her live course to a recorded video series, and began marketing it using YouTube. In less than four years, Kathy has become a sought-after expert in her niche.

Kathy has developed a loyal following, has over one million views on her YouTube channel, and is a master at driving traffic.

www.ingramcontent.com/pod-product-compliance
Lightning Source LLC
Chambersburg PA
CBHW060621200326
41521CB00007B/847